Penguin University Books
The Social Reality of Religion

Peter L. Berger is Professor of Sociology at Rutgers
University, New Brunswick, New Jersey. He has
become well known in America as a proponent of a
'humanistic' approach in sociology. His other works
published in England include *Invitation to Sociology*,
*A Rumour of Angels: Modern Society and the
Rediscovery of the Supernatural* and *The Social
Construction of Reality* (with Thomas Luckmann – a
Penguin University Book).

Peter L. Berger

The Social Reality
of Religion

Penguin Books

Penguin Books Ltd, Harmondsworth,
Middlesex, England
Penguin Books Australia Ltd, Ringwood,
Victoria, Australia

First published in the U.S.A. as
The Sacred Canopy 1967
Published in Great Britain by
Faber & Faber 1969
Published in
Penguin University Books 1973

Copyright © Peter L. Berger, 1967

Printed in Great Britain by
Fletcher & Son Ltd, Norwich
and bound by Richard Clay
(The Chaucer Press) Ltd, Bungay, Suffolk
Set in Intertype Plantin

Contents

Preface

The following argument is intended to be an exercise in sociological theory. Specifically, it seeks to apply a general theoretical
perspective derived from the sociology of knowledge to the
phenomenon of religion. While at certain points the argument
moves on levels of considerable abstraction, it never leaves (at
least not intentionally) the frame of reference of the empirical
discipline of sociology. Consequently, it must rigidly bracket
throughout any questions of the ultimate truth or illusion of
religious propositions about the world. There is neither explicit
nor implied theology in this argument. The brief comments on
possible implications of this perspective for the theologian made
in Appendix II are not necessary to the argument and do not
logically grow out of it. They were motivated by a personal
affection for theologians and their enterprise that need not
trouble the theologically uninterested reader of this book. What
undoubtedly will trouble some sociologists, especially in America, is the closeness of some of the argument to philosophical
considerations, which may seem to them extraneous to sociology proper. This, I suppose, cannot be helped. This book is not
the place to argue through the relationship between sociological
theory and philosophy, so all I can do here is to plead for a spirit
of ecumenical tolerance on the part of my fellow sociologists
(something, incidentally, where they could profitably learn from
recent theology).

It should also be stressed that this book is not 'a sociology of
religion'. An enterprise worthy of this name would have to deal
with vast materials not even touched upon here – such as the
relationship between religion and other institutions in society, the

forms of religious institutionalization, the types of religious leadership, and so forth. The present argument, as an exercise in sociological theorizing, has a much more modest aim.

Essentially, what I have tried to do here is to push to the final sociological consequence an understanding of religion as a historical product. Both my indebtedness to and my divergences from the classical Marxian, Weberian, and Durkheimian approaches to religion will be noted where appropriate. I have not felt it necessary to propose a radically sociological definition of religion, but have operated with the conventional conception of the phenomenon common to the history of religions and to *Religionswissenschaft* generally. My reasons for this are briefly stated in Appendix I.

The argument falls into two parts, a systematic and a historical one. Only the former is, strictly speaking, the afore-mentioned theoretical exercise. What I have tried to do in the second part, on the hand of a discussion of modern secularization, is to show the 'pay-off' of the theoretical perspective in terms of an understanding of specific socio-historical situations. The notes are intended to indicate my theoretical sources, as well as to show what historical and empirical materials have been utilized. I have been careful to 'pay all my debts', but it will be clear that no attempt has been made to convert the footnotes into a general bibliography for the sociology of religion, which would have been quite inappropriate here in terms of the intention of the argument itself.

This book bears a special relationship to *The Social Construction of Reality – A Treatise in the Sociology of Knowledge* (1966), which I wrote together with Thomas Luckmann. Especially chapters 1 and 2 of the present book are a direct application of the same theoretical perspective in the sociology of knowledge to the phenomenon of religion. It would have been very tedious to make cross references to *The Social Construction of Reality* throughout the present book, so I will limit myself to this general reference here. It goes without saying that Luckmann is in no way to be held responsible for what follows. While there may be honour among thieves as well as among sociologists of knowledge, some crimes are committed together and some separately.

It seems that, whenever I find the need to make personal acknowledgements in connection with things I have done in recent years, I always end up mentioning more or less the same people. This is a little boring, but at the same time serves to dispel anomic feelings. In anything that has to do with the sociology of religion I owe the profoundest gratitude to my teacher Carl Mayer. My debt to Thomas Luckmann far exceeds the limits of the particular undertakings that have emerged in print under both our names. Conversations with Brigitte Berger and Hansfried Kellner about these and related matters have left their imprint on my thinking. My communication with denizens of the realm of theology has, much to my regret, shrunk in recent years. But I would like to mention James Gustafson and Siegfried von Kortzfleisch as two theologians in whom I have always found an unusual openness to sociological thinking for which I have been grateful on more than one occasion.

New York   P.L.B.

PART I

Systematic Elements

Religion and World-Construction

Every human society is an enterprise of world-building. Religion occupies a distinctive place in this enterprise. Our main purpose here is to make some general statements about the relationship between human religion and human world-building. Before this can be done intelligibly, however, the above statement about the world-building efficacy of society must be explicated. For this explication it will be important to understand society in dialectic terms.[1]

Society is a dialectic phenomenon in that it is a human product, and nothing but a human product, that yet continuously acts back upon its producer. Society is a product of man. It has no other being except that which is bestowed upon it by human activity and consciousness. There can be no social reality apart from man. Yet it may also be stated that man is a product of society. Every individual biography is an episode within the history of society, which both precedes and survives it. Society was there before the individual was born and it will be there after he has died. What is more, it is within society, and as a result of social processes, that the individual becomes a person, that he attains and holds on to an identity, and that he carries out the various projects that constitute his life. Man cannot exist apart from society. The two statements, that society is the product of man and that man is the product of society, are not contradictory. They rather reflect the inherently dialectic character of the societal phenomenon. Only if this character is recognized will society be understood in terms that are adequate to its empirical reality.[2]

The fundamental dialectic process of society consists of three moments, or steps. These are externalization, objectivation, and internalization. Only if these three moments are understood together can an empirically adequate view of society be maintained. Externalization is the ongoing outpouring of human being into the world, both in the physical and the mental activity of men. Objectivation is the attainment by the products of this activity (again both physical and mental) of a reality that confronts its original producers as a facticity external to and other than themselves. Internalization is the reappropriation by men of this same reality, transforming it once again from structures of the objective world into structures of the subjective consciousness. It is through externalization that society is a human product. It is through objectivation that society becomes a reality *sui generis*. It is through internalization that man is a product of society.[3]

Externalization is an anthropological necessity. Man, as we know him empirically, cannot be conceived of apart from the continuous outpouring of himself into the world in which he finds himself. Human being cannot be understood as somehow resting within itself in some closed sphere of interiority, and *then* setting out to express itself in the surrounding world. Human being is externalizing in its essence and from the beginning.[4] This anthropological root fact is very probably grounded in the biological constitution of man.[5] *Homo sapiens* occupies a peculiar position in the animal kingdom. This peculiarity manifests itself in man's relationship both to his own body and to the world. Unlike the other higher mammals, who are born with an essentially completed organism, man is curiously 'unfinished' at birth.[6] Essential steps in the process of 'finishing' man's development, which have already taken place in the foetal period for the other higher mammals, occur in the first year after birth in the case of man. That is, the biological process of 'becoming man' occurs at a time when the human infant is in interaction with an extraorganismic environment, which includes both the physical and the human world of the infant. There is thus a biological foundation to the process of 'becoming man' in the sense of developing personality and appropriating culture. The latter developments are not somehow superimposed as alien mutations upon the biological development of man, but they are grounded in it

The 'unfinished' character of the human organism at birth is closely related to the relatively unspecialized character of its instinctual structure. The non-human animal enters the world with highly specialized and firmly directed drives. As a result, it lives in a world that is more or less completely determined by its instinctual structure. This world is closed in terms of its possibilities, programmed, as it were, by the animal's own constitution. Consequently, each animal lives in an environment that is specific to its particular species. There is a mouse-world, a dog-world, a horse-world, and so forth. By contrast, man's instinctual structure at birth is both underspecialized and undirected towards a species-specific environment. There is no man-world in the above sense. Man's world is imperfectly programmed by his own constitution. It is an open world. That is, it is a world that must be fashioned by man's own activity. Compared with the other higher mammals, man thus has a double relationship to the world. Like the other mammals, man is *in* a world that antedates his appearance. But unlike the other mammals, this world is not simply given, prefabricated for him. Man must *make* a world for himself. The world-building activity of man, therefore, is not a biologically extraneous phenomenon, but the direct consequence of man's biological constitution.

The condition of the human organism in the world is thus characterized by a built-in instability. Man does not have a given relationship to the world. He must ongoingly establish a relationship with it. The same instability marks man's relationship to his own body.[7] In a curious way, man is 'out of balance' with himself. He cannot rest within himself, but must continuously come to terms with himself by expressing himself in activity. Human existence is an ongoing 'balancing act' between man and his body, man and his world. One may put this differently by saying that man is constantly in the process of 'catching up with himself'. It is in this process that man produces a world. Only in such a world produced by himself can he locate himself and realize his life. But the same process that builds his world also 'finishes' his own being. In other words, man not only produces a world, but he also produces himself. More precisely, he produces himself in a world.

In the process of world-building, man, by his own activity, specializes his drives and provides stability for himself. Biologically deprived of a man-world, he constructs a human world. This world, of course, is culture. Its fundamental purpose is to provide the firm structures for human life that are lacking biologically. It follows that these humanly produced structures can never have the stability that marks the structures of the animal world. Culture, although it becomes for man a 'second nature', remains something quite different from nature precisely because it is the product of man's own activity. Culture must be continuously produced and reproduced by man. Its structures are, therefore, inherently precarious and predestined to change. The cultural imperative of stability and the inherent character of culture as *un*stable together posit the fundamental problem of man's world-building activity. Its far-reaching implications will occupy us in considerable detail a little further on. For the moment, suffice it to say that, while it is necessary that worlds be built, it is quite difficult to keep them going.

Culture consists of the totality of man's products.[8] Some of these are material, others are not. Man produces tools of every conceivable kind, by means of which he modifies his physical environment and bends nature to his will. Man also produces language and, on its foundation and by means of it, a towering edifice of symbols that permeate every aspect of his life. There is good reason for thinking that the production of non-material culture has always gone hand in hand with man's activity of physically modifying his environment.[9] Be this as it may, society is, of course, nothing but part and parcel of non-material culture. Society is that aspect of the latter that structures man's ongoing relations with his fellow men.[10] As but an element of culture, society fully shares in the latter's character as a human product. Society is constituted and maintained by human beings. It has no being, no reality, apart from this activity. Its patterns, always relative in time and space, are not given in nature, nor can they be deduced in any specific manner from the 'nature of man'. If one wants to use such a term as designating more than certain biological constants, one can only say that it is the 'nature of man' to produce a world. What appears at any particular historical moment as 'human nature' is itself a product of man's world-building activity.[11]

However, while society appears as but an aspect of culture, it occupies a privileged position among man's cultural formations. This is due to yet another basic anthropological fact, namely the essential sociality of man.[12] *Homo sapiens* is the social animal. This means very much more than the surface fact that man always lives in collectivities and, indeed, loses his humanity when he is thrust into isolation from other men. Much more importantly, the world-building activity of man is always and inevitably a collective enterprise. While it may be possible, perhaps for heuristic purposes, to analyse man's relationship to his world in purely individual terms, the empirical reality of human world-building is always a social one. Men *together* shape tools, invent languages, adhere to values, devise institutions, and so on. Not only is the individual's participation in a culture contingent upon a social process (namely, the process called socialization), but his continuing cultural existence depends upon the maintenance of specific social arrangements. Society, therefore, is not only an outcome of culture, but a necessary condition of the latter. Society structures, distributes, and coordinates the world-building activities of men. And only in society can the products of those activities persist over time.

The understanding of society as rooted in man's externalization, that is, as a product of human activity, is particularly important in view of the fact that society appears to common sense as something quite different, as independent of human activity and as sharing in the inert givenness of nature. We shall turn in a moment to the process of objectivation that makes this appearance possible. Suffice it to say here that one of the most important gains of a sociological perspective is its reiterated reduction of the hypostatized entities that make up society in the imagination of the man in the street to the human activity of which these entities are products and without which they have no status in reality. The 'stuff' out of which society and all its formations are made is human meanings externalized in human activity. The great societal hypostases (such as 'the family', 'the economy', 'the state', and so forth) are over again reduced by sociological analysis to the human activity that is their only underlying substance. For this reason it is very unhelpful if the sociologist, except for heuristic purposes, deals with such social phenomena as if they were, in actual fact, hypostases independent of the human enterprise that originally produced them and keeps on producing them. There is nothing wrong, in itself, with the sociologist's speaking of institutions, structures, functions, patterns, and so on. The harm comes only when he thinks of these, like the man in the street, as entities existing in and of themselves, detached from human activity and production. One of the merits of the concept of externalization, as applied to society, is the prevention of this sort of static, hypostatizing thinking. Another way of putting this is to say that sociological understanding ought always to be humanizing, that is, ought to refer back the imposing configurations of social structure to the living human beings who have created them.[13]

Society, then, is a product of man, rooted in the phenomenon of externalization, which in turn is grounded in the very biological constitution of man. As soon as one speaks of externalized products, however, one is implying that the latter attain a degree of distinctiveness as against their producer. This transformation of man's products into a world that not only derives from man, but that comes to confront him as a facticity outside of himself, is intended in the concept of objectivation. The humanly produced world becomes something 'out there'. It consists of objects, both material and non-material, that are capable of resisting the desires of their producer. Once produced, this world cannot simply be wished away. Although all culture originates and is rooted in the subjective consciousness of human beings, once formed it cannot be reabsorbed into consciousness at will. It stands outside the subjectivity of the individual as, indeed, a world. In other words, the humanly produced world attains the character of objective reality.

This acquired objectivity of man's cultural products pertains both to the material and the non-material ones. It can readily be understood in the case of the former. Man manufactures a tool and by that action enriches the totality of physical objects present in the world. Once produced, the tool has a being of its own that cannot be readily changed by those who employ it. Indeed, the tool (say, an agricultural implement) may even enforce the logic of its being upon its users, sometimes in a way that may not be particularly agreeable to them. For instance, a plough, though obviously a human product, is an external object not only in the sense that its users may fall over it and hurt themselves as a result, just as they may be falling over a rock or a stump or any other natural object. More interestingly, the plough may compel its users to arrange their agricultural activity, and perhaps also other aspects of their lives, in a way that conforms to *its* own logic and that may have been neither intended nor foreseen by those who originally devised it. The same objectivity, however, characterizes the non-material elements of culture as well. Man invents a language and then finds that both his speaking and his thinking are dominated by its grammar. Man produces values and discovers that he feels guilt when he contravenes them. Man concocts institutions, which come to confront him as powerfully controlling and even menacing constellations of the external world. The relationship between man and culture is thus aptly illustrated by the tale of the sorcerer's apprentice. The mighty buckets, magically called out of nothingness by human *fiat*, are set in motion. From that point on they go about drawing water in accordance with an inherent logic of their own being that, at the very least, is less than completely controlled by their creator. It is possible, as happens in that story, that man may find an additional magic that will bring back under his control the vast forces he has unleashed upon reality. This power, though, is not identical with the one that first set these forces in motion. And, of course, it can also happen that man drowns in the floods that he himself has produced.

If culture is credited with the status of objectivity, there is a double meaning to this appellation. Culture is objective in that it confronts man as an assemblage of objects in the real world existing outside his own consciousness. Culture is *there*. But culture is also objective in that it may be experienced and apprehended, as it were, in company. Culture is *there for everybody*. This means that the objects of culture (again, both the material and non-material ones) may be shared with others. This distinguishes them sharply from any constructions of the subjective consciousness of the solitary individual. This is obvious when one compares a tool that belongs to the technology of a particular culture with some utensil, however interesting, that forms part of a dream. The objectivity of culture as shared facticity, though, is even more important to understand with reference to its non-material constituents. The individual may dream up any number of, say, institutional arrangements that might well be more interesting, perhaps even more functional, than the institutions actually recognized in his culture. As long as these sociological dreams, so to speak, are confined to the individual's own consciousness and are not recognized by others as at least empirical possibilities, they will exist only as shadowlike phantasmata. By contrast, the institutions of the individual's society, however much he may dislike them, will be *real*. In other words, the cultural world is not only collectively produced, but it remains real by virtue of collective recognition. To be in culture means to share in a particular world of objectivities with others.[14]

The same conditions, of course, apply to that segment of cultures we call society. It is not enough, therefore, to say that society is rooted in human activity. One must also say that society is *objectivated* human activity, that is, society is a product of human activity that has attained the status of objective reality. The social formations are experienced by man as elements of an objective world. Society confronts man as external, subjectively opaque and coercive facticity.[15] Indeed, society is commonly apprehended by man as virtually equivalent to the physical universe in its objective presence – a 'second nature', indeed. Society is experienced as given 'out there', extraneous to subjective consciousness and not controllable by the latter. The representations of solitary fantasy offer relatively little resistance to the individual's volition. The representations of society are immensely more resistant. The individual can dream of different societies and imagine himself in various contexts. Unless he exists in solipsistic madness, he will know the difference between these fantasies and the *reality* of his actual life in society, which prescribes a commonly recognized context for him and imposes it upon him regardless of his wishes. Since society is encountered by the individual as a reality external to himself, it may often happen that its workings remain opaque to his understanding. He cannot discover the meaning of a social phenomenon by introspection. He must, for this purpose, go outside himself and engage in the basically same kind of empirical inquiry that is necessary if he is to understand anything located outside his own mind. Above all, society manifests itself by its coercive power. The final test of its objective reality is its capacity to impose itself upon the reluctance of individuals. Society directs, sanctions, controls, and punishes individual conduct. In its most powerful apotheoses (not a loosely chosen term, as we shall see later), society may even destroy the individual.

The coercive objectivity of society can, of course, be seen most readily in its procedures of social control, that is, in those procedures that are specifically designed to 'bring back into line' recalcitrant individuals or groups. Political and legal institutions may serve as obvious illustrations of this. It is important to understand, however, that the same coercive objectivity characterizes society *as a whole* and is present in *all* social institutions, including those institutions that were founded on consensus. This (most emphatically) does *not* mean that all societies are variations of tyranny. It *does* mean that no human construction can be accurately called a social phenomenon unless it has achieved that measure of objectivity that compels the individual to recognize it as real. In other words, the fundamental coerciveness of society lies not in its machineries of social control, but in its power to constitute and to impose itself as reality. The paradigmatic case of this is language. Hardly anyone, however far removed from sociological thinking, is likely to deny that language is a human product. Any particular language is the result of a long history of human inventiveness, imagination and even caprice. While man's vocal organs impose certain physiological limitations on his linguistic fancy, there are no laws of nature that can be called upon to explain the development of, say, the English language. Nor does the latter have any status in the nature of things other than its status as a human production. The English language originated in specific human events, was developed throughout its history by human activity, and it exists only in so far and as long as human beings continue to use and understand it. Nevertheless, the English language presents itself to the individual as an objective reality, which he must recognize as such or suffer the consequences. Its rules are objectively given. They must be learned by the individual, whether as his first or as a foreign language, and he cannot change them at will. There are objective standards for correct and incorrect English, and although there may be differences of opinion about minor details, the existence of such standards is a precondition for the use of the language in the first place. There are, of course, penalties for offending against these standards, from failing in school to social embarrassment in later life, but the objective reality of the English language is not primarily constituted by these penalties. Rather, the English language is real objectively by virtue of the simple fact that it is *there*, a ready-made and collectively recognized universe of discourse within which individuals may understand each other and themselves.[16]

Society, as objective reality, provides a world for man to inhabit. This world encompasses the biography of the individual, which unfolds as a series of events *within* that world. Indeed, the individual's own biography is objectively real only in so far as it may be comprehended within the significant structures of the social world. To be sure, the individual may have any number of highly subjective self-interpretations, which will strike others as bizarre or as downright incomprehensible. Whatever these self-interpretations may be, there will remain the objective interpretation of the individual's biography that locates the latter in a collectively recognized frame of reference. The objective facts of this biography may be minimally ascertained by consulting the relevant personal documents. Name, legal descent, citizenship, civil status, occupation – these are but some of the 'official' interpretations of individual existence, objectively valid not only by force of law but by the fundamental reality-bestowing potency of society. What is more, the individual himself, unless again he encloses himself in a solipsistic world of withdrawal from the common reality, will seek to validate his self-interpretations by comparing them with the objectively available coordinates of his biography. In other words, the individual's own life appears as objectively real, to himself as well as to others, only as it is located within a social world that itself has the character of objective reality.[17]

The objectivity of society extends to all its constituent elements. Institutions, roles, and identities exist as objectively real phenomena in the social world, though they and this world are at the same time nothing but human productions. For example, the family as the institutionalization of human sexuality in a particular society is experienced and apprehended as an objective reality. The institution is *there,* external and coercive, imposing its predefined patterns upon the individual in this particular area of his life. The same objectivity belongs to the roles that the individual is expected to play in the institutional context in question, even if it should happen that he does not particularly enjoy the performance. The roles of, for instance, husband, father or uncle are objectively defined and available as models for individual conduct. By playing these roles, the individual comes to represent the institutional objectivities in a way that is apprehended, by himself and by others, as detached from the 'mere' accidents of his individual existence.[18] He can 'put on' the role, as a cultural object, in a manner analogous to the 'putting on' of a physical object of clothing or adornment. He can further retain a consciousness of himself as distinct from the role, which then relates to what he apprehends as his 'real self' as mask to actor. Thus he can even say that he does not like to perform this or that detail of the role, but must do so against his will – because the objective description of the role so dictates. Furthermore, society not only contains an objectively available assemblage of institutions and roles, but a repertoire of identities endowed with the same status of objective reality. Society assigns to the individual not only a set of roles but a designated identity. In other words, the individual is not only expected to perform as husband, father, or uncle, but to *be* a husband, a father, or an uncle – and, even more basically, to *be* a man, in terms of whatever 'being' this implies in the society in question. Thus, in the final resort, the objectivation of human activity means that man becomes capable of objectivating a part of himself within his own consciousness, confronting himself within himself in figures that are generally available as objective elements of the social world. For example, the individual *qua* 'real self' can carry on an internal conversation with himself *qua* archbishop. Actually, it is only by means of such internal dialogue with the objectivations of oneself that socialization is possible in the first place.[19]

The world of social objectivations, produced by externalizing consciousness, confronts consciousness as an external facticity. It is apprehended as such. This apprehension, however, cannot as yet be described as internalization, any more than can the apprehension of the world of nature. Internalization is rather the reabsorption into consciousness of the objectivated world in such a way that the structures of this world come to determine the subjective structures of consciousness itself. That is, society now functions as the formative agency for individual consciousness. In so far as internalization has taken place, the individual now apprehends various elements of the objectivated world as phenomena internal to his consciousness at the same time as he apprehends them as phenomena of external reality.

Every society that continues in time faces the problem of transmitting its objectivated meanings from one generation to the next. This problem is attacked by means of the processes of socialization, that is, the processes by which a new generation is taught to live in accordance with the institutional programmes of the society. Socialization can, of course, be described psychologically as a learning process. The new generation is initiated into the meanings of the culture, learns to participate in its established tasks and to accept the roles as well as the identities that make up its social structure. Socialization, however, has a crucial dimension that is not adequately grasped by speaking of a learning process. The individual not only learns the objectivated meanings but identifies with and is shaped by them. He draws them into himself and makes them *his* meanings. He becomes not only one who possesses these meanings, but one who represents and expresses them.

The success of socialization depends upon the establishment of symmetry between the objective world of society and the subjective world of the individual. If one imagines a totally socialized individual, each meaning objectively available in the social world would have its analogous meaning given subjectively within his own consciousness. Such total socialization is empirically non-existent and theoretically impossible, if only by reason of the biological variability of individuals. However, there are degrees of success in socialization. Highly successful socialization establishes a high degree of objective/subjective symmetry, while failures of socialization lead to various degrees of asymmetry. If socialization is not successful in internalizing at least the most important meanings of a given society, the latter becomes difficult to maintain as a viable enterprise. Specifically, such a society would not be in a position to establish a tradition that would ensure its persistence in time.

Man's world-building activity is always a collective enterprise. Man's internal appropriation of a world must also take place in a collectivity. It has by now become a social-scientific platitude to say that it is impossible to become or to be human, in any empirically recognizable form that goes beyond biological observations, except in society. This becomes less of a platitude if one adds that the internalization of a world is dependent on society in the same way, because one is thereby saying that man is incapable of conceiving of his experience in a comprehensively meaningful way unless such a conception is transmitted to him by means of social processes. The processes that internalize the socially objectivated world are *the same* processes that internalize the socially assigned identities. The individual is socialized *to be* a designated person and *to inhabit* a designated world. Subjective identity and subjective reality are produced in the same dialectic (here, in the etymologically literal sense) between the individual and those significant others who are in charge of his social-ization.[20] It is possible to sum up the dialectic formation of identity by saying that the individual becomes that which he is addressed as by others. One may add that the individual appro-priates the world in conversation with others and, furthermore, that both identity and world remain real to himself only as long as he can continue the conversation.

The last point is very important, for it implies that social-ization can never be completed, that it must be an ongoing process throughout the lifetime of the individual. This is the subjective side of the already remarked-upon precariousness of all humanly constructed worlds. The difficulty of keeping a world going expresses itself psychologically in the difficulty of keeping this world subjectively plausible. The world is built up in the consciousness of the individual by conversation with significant others (such as parents, teachers, 'peers'). The world is maintained as subjective reality by the same sort of conversation, be it with the same or with new significant others (such as spouses, friends, or other associates). If such conversation is dis-rupted (the spouse dies, the friends disappear, or one comes to leave one's original social milieu), the world begins to totter, to lose its subjective plausibility. In other words, the subjective re-ality of the world hangs on the thin thread of conversation. The reason why most of us are unaware of this precariousness most of the time is grounded in the continuity of our conversation with significant others. The maintenance of such continuity is one of the most important imperatives of social order.

Internalization, then, implies that the objective facticity of the social world becomes a subjective facticity as well. The individual encounters the institutions as *data* of the objective world outside himself, but they are now *data* of his own consciousness as well. The institutional programmes set up by society are subjectively real as attitudes, motives and life projects. The reality of the institutions is appropriated by the individual along with his roles and his identity. For example, the individual appropriates as reality the particular kinship arrangements of his society. *Ipso facto,* he takes on the roles assigned to him in this context and apprehends his own identity in terms of these roles. Thus, he not only plays the role of uncle, but he *is* an uncle. Nor, if socialization has been fairly successful, does he wish to be anything else. His attitudes towards others and his motives for specific actions are endemically avuncular. If he lives in a society which has established unclehood as a centrally significant institution (not ours, to be sure, but most matrilineal societies), he will conceive of his whole biography (past, present, *and* future) in terms of his career *as* an uncle. Indeed, he may even sacrifice himself for his nephews and derive consolation from the thought that his own life will continue in them. The socially objectivated world is still apprehended as external facticity. Uncles, sisters, nephews exist in objective reality, comparable in facticity to the species of animals or rocks. But this objective world is also apprehended now as subjective meaningfulness. Its initial opaqueness (say, to the child, who must learn the lore of unclehood) has been converted to an internal translucency. The individual may now look within himself and, in the depths of his subjective being, may 'discover himself' as an uncle. At this point, always assuming a degree of successful socialization, introspection becomes a viable method for the discovery of institutional meanings.[21]

The process of internalization must always be understood as but one moment of the larger dialectic process that also includes the moments of externalization and objectivation. If this is not done there emerges a picture of mechanistic determinism, in which the individual is produced by society as cause produces effect in nature. Such a picture distorts the societal phenomenon. Not only is internalization part of the latter's larger dialectic, but the socialization of the individual also occurs in a dialectic manner.[22] The individual is not moulded as a passive, inert thing. Rather, he is formed in the course of a protracted conversation (a dialectic, in the literal sense of the word) in which he is a *participant*. That is, the social world (with its appropriate institutions, roles, and identities) is not passively absorbed by the individual, but actively *appropriated* by him. Furthermore, once the individual is formed as a person, with an objectively and subjectively recognizable identity, he must continue to participate in the conversation that sustains him as a person in his ongoing biography. That is, the individual continues to be a *co-producer* of the social world, and thus of himself. No matter how small his power to change the social definitions of reality may be, he must at least continue to assent to those that form him as a person. Even if he should deny this co-production (say, as a positivistic sociologist or psychologist), he remains a co-producer of his world all the same – and, indeed, his denial of this enters into the dialectic as a formative factor both of his world and of himself. The relationship of the individual to language may, once more, be taken as paradigmatic of the dialectic of socialization. Language confronts the individual as an objective facticity. He subjectively appropriates it by engaging in linguistic interaction with others. In the course of this interaction, however, he inevitably modifies the language, even if (say, as a formalistic grammarian) he should deny the validity of these modifications. Furthermore, his continuing participation in the language is part of the human activity that is the only ontological base for the language in question. The language exists because he, along with others, continues to employ it. In other words, both with regard to language and to the socially objectivated world as a whole, it may be said that the individual keeps 'talking back' to the world that formed him and thereby continues to maintain the latter as reality.

It may now be understandable if the proposition is made that the socially constructed world is, above all, an ordering of experience. A meaningful order, or nomos, is imposed upon the discrete experiences and meanings of individuals.[23] To say that society is a world-building enterprise is to say that it is ordering, or nomizing, activity. The presupposition for this is given, as has been indicated before, in the biological constitution of *homo sapiens*. Man, biologically denied the ordering mechanisms with which the other animals are endowed, is compelled to impose his own order upon experience. Man's sociality presupposes the collective character of this ordering activity. The ordering of experience is endemic to any kind of social interaction. Every social action implies that individual meaning is directed towards others and ongoing social interaction implies that the several meanings of the actors are integrated into an order of common meaning.[24] It would be wrong to assume that this nomizing consequence of social interaction must, from the beginning, produce a nomos that embraces *all* the discrete experiences and meanings of the participant individuals. If one can imagine a society in its first origins (something, of course, that is empirically unavailable), one may assume that the range of the common nomos expands as social interaction comes to include ever broader areas of common meaning. It makes no sense to imagine that this nomos will ever include the totality of individual meanings. Just as there can be no totally socialized individuals, so there will always be individual meanings that remain outside of or marginal to the common nomos. Indeed, as will be seen a little later, the marginal experiences of the individual are of considerable importance for an understanding of social existence. All the same, there is an inherent logic that impels every nomos to expand into wider areas of meaning. If the ordering activity of society never attains to totality, it may yet be described as totalizing.[25]

The social world constitutes a nomos both objectively and subjectively. The objective nomos is given in the process of objectivation as such. The fact of language, even if taken by itself, can readily be seen as the imposition of order upon experience. Language nomizes by imposing differentiation and structure upon the ongoing flux of experience. As an item of experience is named, it is *ipso facto*, taken out of this flux and given stability *as* the entity so named. Language further provides a fundamental order of relationships by the addition of syntax and grammar to vocabulary. It is impossible to use language without participating in its order. Every empirical language may be said to constitute a nomos in the making, or, with equal validity, as the historical consequence of the nomizing activity of generations of men. The original nomizing act is to say that an item is *this,* and thus *not that*. As this original incorporation of the item into an order that includes other items is followed by sharper linguistic designations (the item is male and not female, singular and not plural, a noun and not a verb, and so forth), the nomizing act intends a comprehensive order of *all* items that may be linguistically objectivated, that is, intends a totalizing nomos.

On the foundation of language, and by means of it, is built up the cognitive and normative edifice that passes for 'knowledge' in a society. In what it 'knows', every society imposes a common order of interpretation upon experience that becomes 'objective knowledge' by means of the process of objectivation discussed before. Only a relatively small part of this edifice is constituted by theories of one kind or another, though theoretical 'knowledge' is particularly important because it usually contains the body of 'official' interpretations of reality. Most socially objectivated 'knowledge' is pretheoretical. It consists of interpretative schemas, moral maxims and collections of traditional wisdom that the man in the street frequently shares with the theoreticians. Societies vary in the degree of differentiation in their bodies of 'knowledge'. Whatever these variations, every society provides for its members an objectively available body of 'knowledge'. To participate in the society is to share its 'knowledge', that is, to co-inhabit its nomos.

The objective nomos is internalized in the course of socialization. It is thus appropriated by the individual to become his own subjective ordering of experience. It is by virtue of this appropriation that the individual can come to 'make sense' of his own biography. The discrepant elements of his past life are ordered in terms of what he 'knows objectively' about his own and others' condition. His ongoing experience is integrated into the same order, though the latter may have to be modified to allow for this integration. The future attains a meaningful shape by virtue of the same order being projected into it. In other words, to live in the social world is to live an ordered and meaningful life. Society is the guardian of order and meaning not only objectively, in its institutional structures, but subjectively as well, in its structuring of individual consciousness.

It is for this reason that radical separation from the social world, or anomy, constitutes such a powerful threat to the individual.[26] It is not only that the individual loses emotionally satisfying ties in such cases. He loses his orientation in experience. In extreme cases, he loses his sense of reality and identity. He becomes anomic in the sense of becoming worldless. Just as an individual's nomos is constructed and sustained in conversation with significant others, so is the individual plunged towards anomy when such conversation is radically interrupted. The circumstances of such nomic disruption may, of course, vary. They might involve large collective forces, such as the loss of status of the entire social group to which the individual belongs. They might be more narrowly biographical, such as the loss of significant others by death, divorce, or physical separation. It is thus possible to speak of collective as well as of individual states of anomy. In both cases, the fundamental order in terms of which the individual can 'make sense' of his life and recognize his own identity will be in process of disintegration. Not only will the individual then begin to lose his moral bearings, with disastrous psychological consequences, but he will become uncertain about his cognitive bearings as well. The world begins to shake in the very instant that its sustaining conversation begins to falter.

The socially established nomos may thus be understood, perhaps in its most important aspect, as a shield against terror. Put differently, the most important function of society is nomization. The anthropological presupposition for this is a human craving for meaning that appears to have the force of instinct. Men are congenitally compelled to impose a meaningful order upon reality. This order, however, presupposes the social enterprise of ordering world-construction. To be separated from society exposes the individual to a multiplicity of dangers with which he is unable to cope by himself, in the extreme case to the danger of imminent extinction. Separation from society also inflicts unbearable psychological tensions upon the individual, tensions that are grounded in the root anthropological fact of sociality. The ultimate danger of such separation, however, is the danger of meaninglessness. This danger is the nightmare *par excellence*, in which the individual is submerged in a world of disorder, senselessness and madness. Reality and identity are malignantly transformed into meaningless figures of horror. To be in society is to be 'sane' precisely in the sense of being shielded from the ultimate 'insanity' of such anomic terror. Anomy is unbearable to the point where the individual may seek death in preference to it. Conversely, existence within a nomic world may be sought at the cost of all sorts of sacrifice and suffering – and even at the cost of life itself, if the individual believes that this ultimate sacrifice has nomic significance.[27]

The sheltering quality of social order becomes especially evident if one looks at the marginal situations in the life of the individual, that is, at situations in which he is driven close to or beyond the boundaries of the order that determines his routine, everyday existence.[28] Such marginal situations commonly occur in dreams and fantasy. They may appear on the horizon of consciousness as haunting suspicions that the world may have another aspect than its 'normal' one, that is, that the previously accepted definitions of reality may be fragile or even fraudulent.[29] Such suspicions extend to the identity of both self and others, positing the possibility of shattering metamorphoses. When these suspicions invade the central areas of consciousness they take on, of course, the constellations that modern psychiatry would call neurotic or psychotic. Whatever the epistemological status of these constellations (usually decided upon much too sanguinely by psychiatry, precisely because it is firmly rooted in the everyday, 'official', social definitions of reality), their profound terror for the individual lies in the threat they constitute to his previously operative nomos. The marginal situation *par excellence*, however, is death.[30] Witnessing the death of others (notably, of course, of significant others) and anticipating his own death, the individual is strongly propelled to question the *ad hoc* cognitive and normative operating procedures of his 'normal' life in society. Death presents society with a formidable problem not only because of its obvious threat to the continuity of human relationships, but because it threatens the basic assumptions of order on which society rests.

In other words, the marginal situations of human existence reveal the innate precariousness of all social worlds. Every socially defined reality remains threatened by lurking 'irrealities'. Every socially constructed nomos must face the constant possibility of its collapse into anomy. Seen in the perspective of society, every nomos is an area of meaning carved out of a vast mass of meaninglessness, a small clearing of lucidity in a formless, dark, always ominous jungle. Seen in the perspective of the individual, every nomos represents the bright 'dayside' of life, tenuously held on to against the sinister shadows of the 'night'. In both perspectives, every nomos is an edifice erected in the face of the potent and alien forces of chaos. This chaos must be kept at bay at all costs. To ensure this, every society develops procedures that assist its members to remain 'reality-oriented' (that is, to remain within the reality as 'officially' defined) and to 'return to reality' (that is, to return from the marginal spheres of 'irreality' to the socially established nomos). These procedures will have to be looked at more closely a little later. For the moment, suffice it to say that the individual is provided by society with various methods to stave off the nightmare world of anomy and to stay within the safe boundaries of the established nomos.

The social world intends, as far as possible, to be taken for granted.[31] Socialization achieves success to the degree that this taken-for-granted quality is internalized. It is not enough that the individual look upon the key meanings of the social order as useful, desirable, or right. It is much better (better, that is, in terms of social stability) if he looks upon them as inevitable, as part and parcel of the universal 'nature of things'. If that can be achieved, the individual who strays seriously from the socially defined programmes can be considered not only a fool or a knave, but a madman. Subjectively, then, serious deviance provokes not only moral guilt but the terror of madness. For example, the sexual programme of a society is taken for granted not simply as a utilitarian or morally correct arrangement, but as an inevitable expression of 'human nature'. The so-called 'homosexual panic' may serve as an excellent illustration of the terror unleashed by the denial of the programme. This is not to deny that this terror is also fed by practical apprehensions and qualms of conscience, but its fundamental motorics is the terror of being thrust into an outer darkness that separates one from the 'normal' order of men. In other words, institutional programmes are endowed with an ontological status to the point where to deny them is to deny being itself – the being of the universal order of things and, consequently, one's own being in this order.

Whenever the socially established nomos attains the quality of being taken for granted, there occurs a merging of its meanings with what are considered to be the fundamental meanings inherent in the universe. Nomos and cosmos appear to be co-extensive. In archaic societies, nomos appears as a microcosmic reflection, the world of men as expressing meaning inherent in the universe as such. In contemporary society, this archaic cosmization of the social world is likely to take the form of 'scientific' propositions about the nature of men rather than the nature of the universe.[32] Whatever the historical variations, the tendency is for the meanings of the humanly constructed order to be projected into the universe as such.[33] It may readily be seen how this projection tends to stabilize the tenuous nomic constructions, though the mode of this stabilization will have to be investigated further. In any case, when the nomos is taken for granted as appertaining to the 'nature of things', understood cosmologically *or* anthropologically, it is endowed with a stability deriving from more powerful sources than the historical efforts of human beings. It is at this point that religion enters significantly into our argument.

Religion is the human enterprise by which a sacred cosmos is established.[34] Put differently, religion is cosmization in a sacred mode. By sacred is meant here a quality of mysterious and awesome power, other than man and yet related to him, which is believed to reside in certain objects of experience.[35] This quality may be attributed to natural or artificial objects, to animals, or to men, or to the objectivations of human culture. There are sacred rocks, sacred tools, sacred cows. The chieftain may be sacred, as may be a particular custom or institution. Space and time may be assigned to the same quality, as in sacred localities and sacred seasons. The quality may finally be embodied in sacred beings, from highly localized spirits to the great cosmic divinities. The latter, in turn, may be transformed into ultimate forces or principles ruling the cosmos, no longer conceived of in personal terms but still endowed with the status of sacredness. The historical manifestations of the sacred vary widely, though there are certain uniformities to be observed cross-culturally (no matter here whether these are to be interpreted as resulting from cultural diffusion or from an inner logic of man's religious imagination). The sacred is apprehended as 'sticking out' from the normal routines of everyday life, as something extraordinary and potentially dangerous, though its dangers can be domesticated and its potency harnessed to the needs of everyday life. Although the sacred is apprehended as other than man, yet it refers to man, relating to him in a way in which other non-human phenomena (specifically, the phenomena of non-sacred nature) do not. The cosmos posited by religion thus both transcends and includes man. The sacred cosmos is confronted by man as an immensely powerful reality other than himself. Yet this reality addresses itself to him and locates his life in an ultimately meaningful order.

On one level, the antonym to the sacred is the profane, to be defined simply as the absence of sacred status. All phenomena are profane that do not 'stick out' as sacred. The routines of everyday life are profane unless, so to speak, proven otherwise, in which latter case they are conceived of as being infused in one way or another with sacred power (as in sacred work, for instance). Even in such cases, however, the sacred quality attributed to the ordinary events of life *itself* retains its extraordinary character, a character that is typically reaffirmed through a variety of rituals and the loss of which is tantamount to secularization, that is, to a conception of the events in question as *nothing but* profane. The dichotomization of reality into sacred and profane spheres, however related, is intrinsic to the religious enterprise. As such, it is obviously important for any analysis of the religious phenomenon.

On a deeper level, however, the sacred has another opposed category, that of chaos.[36] The sacred cosmos emerges out of chaos and continues to confront the latter as its terrible contrary. This opposition of cosmos and chaos is frequently expressed in a variety of cosmogonic myths. The sacred cosmos, which transcends and includes man in its ordering of reality, thus provides man's ultimate shield against the terror of anomy. To be in a 'right' relationship with the sacred cosmos is to be protected against the nightmare threats of chaos. To fall out of such a 'right' relationship is to be abandoned on the edge of the abyss of meaninglessness. It is not irrelevant to observe here that the English 'chaos' derives from a Greek word meaning 'yawning' and 'religion' from a Latin one meaning 'to be careful'. To be sure, what the religious man is 'careful' about is above all the dangerous power inherent in the manifestations of the sacred themselves. But behind this danger is the other, much more horrible one, namely that one may lose all connection with the sacred and be swallowed up by chaos. All the nomic constructions, as we have seen, are designed to keep this terror at bay. In the sacred cosmos, however, these constructions achieve their ultimate culmination – literally, their apotheosis.

Human existence is essentially and inevitably externalizing activity. In the course of externalization men pour out meaning into reality. Every human society is an edifice of externalized and objectivated meanings, always intending a meaningful totality. Every society is engaged in the never completed enterprise of building a humanly meaningful world. Cosmization implies the identification of this humanly meaningful world with the world as such, the former now being grounded in the latter, reflecting it or being derived from it in its fundamental structures. Such a cosmos, as the ultimate ground and validation of human nomoi, need not necessarily be sacred. Particularly in modern times there have been thoroughly secular attempts at cosmization, among which modern science is by far the most important. It is safe to say, however, that originally *all* cosmization had a sacred character. This remained true through most of human history, and not only through the millennia of human existence on earth preceding what we now call civilization. Viewed historically, most of man's worlds have been sacred worlds. Indeed, it appears likely that only by way of the sacred was it possible for man to conceive of a cosmos in the first place.[37]

It can thus be said that religion has played a strategic part in the human enterprise of world-building. Religion implies the farthest reach of man's self-externalization, of his infusion of reality with his own meanings. Religion implies that human order is projected into the totality of being. Put differently, religion is the audacious attempt to conceive of the entire universe as being humanly significant.

Religion and World-Maintenance

All socially constructed worlds are inherently precarious. Supported by human activity, they are constantly threatened by the human facts of self-interest and stupidity. The institutional programmes are sabotaged by individuals with conflicting interests. Frequently individuals simply forget them or are incapable of learning them in the first place. The fundamental processes of socialization and social control, to the extent that they are successful, serve to mitigate these threats. Socialization seeks to ensure a continuing consensus concerning the most important features of the social world. Social control seeks to contain individual or group resistances within tolerable limits. There is yet another centrally important process that serves to support the swaying edifice of social order. This is the process of legitimation.[1]

By legitimation, is meant socially objectivated 'knowledge' that serves to explain and justify the social order. Put differently, legitimations are answers to any questions about the 'why' of institutional arrangements. A number of points should be noted about this definition. Legitimations belong to the domain of social objectivations, that is, to what passes for 'knowledge' in a given collectivity. This implies that they have a status of objectivity quite different from merely individual cogitations about the 'why' and 'wherefore' of social events. Legitimations, furthermore, can be both cognitive and normative in character. They do not only tell people what *ought to be*. Often they merely propose what *is*. For instance, the morals of kinship, expressed in a statement such as, 'You ought not to sleep with X, your sister', are obviously legitimating. But cognitive assertions about kinship, such as, 'You are X's brother and she is your sister', are legitimating in an even more fundamental sense. To put it a little crudely, legitimation begins with statements as to 'what's what'. Only on this cognitive basis is it possible for the normative propositions to be meaningful. Finally, it would be a serious mistake to identify legitimation with theoretical ideation.[2] 'Ideas', to be sure, can be important for purposes of legitimation. However, what passes for 'knowledge' in a society is by no means identical with the body of 'ideas' existing in the society. There are always some people with an interest in 'ideas', but they have never yet constituted more than a rather small minority. If legitimation always had to consist of theoretically coherent propositions, it would support the social order only for that minority of intellectuals that have such theoretical interests – obviously not a very practical programme. Most legitimation, consequently, is pre-theoretical in character.

It will be clear from the above that, in one sense, *all* socially objectivated 'knowledge' is legitimating. The nomos of a society first of all legitimates itself by simply being there. Institutions structure human activity. As the meanings of the institutions are nomically integrated, the institutions are *ipso facto* legitimated, to the point where the institutionalized actions appear 'self-evident' to their performers. This level of legitimation is already implied in speaking of the objectivity of social order. In other words, the socially constructed world legitimates itself by virtue of its objective facticity. However, additional legitimations are invariably necessary in any society. This necessity is grounded in the problems of socialization and social control. If the nomos of a society is to be transmitted from one generation to another, so that the new generation will also come to 'inhabit' the same social world, there will have to be legitimating formulas to answer the questions that, inevitably, will arise in the minds of the new generation. Children want to know 'why'. Their teachers must supply convincing answers. Furthermore, as we have seen, socialization is never completed. Not only children but adults as well 'forget' the legitimating answers. They must ever again be 'reminded'. In other words, the legitimating formulas must be repeated. Clearly such repetition will be especially important on those occasions of collective or individual crisis when the danger of 'forgetting' is most acute. Any exercise of social control also demands legitimation over and above the self-legitimating facticity of the institutional arrangements – precisely because this facticity is put in question by the resisters who are to be controlled. The sharper such resistance, and the sharper the means employed to overcome it, the more important will it be to have additional legitimations. Such legitimations serve both to explain why the resistance cannot be tolerated and to justify the means by which it is to be quelled. One may say, then, that the facticity of the social world or of any part of it suffices for self-legitimation as long as there is no challenge. When a challenge appears, in whatever form, the facticity can no longer be taken for granted. The validity of the social order must then be explicated, both for the sake of the challengers and of those meeting the challenge. The children must be convinced, but so must be their teachers. The wrongdoers must be convincingly condemned, but this condemnation must also serve to justify their judges. The seriousness of the challenge will determine the degree of elaborateness of the answering legitimations.

Legitimation occurs, therefore, on a variety of levels. One may first distinguish between the level of self-legitimating facticity and that of, so to speak, secondary legitimations made necessary by challenges to facticity. One may further distinguish between different level of the latter type of legitimations. On the pre-theoretical level there are to be found simple traditional affirmations of which the paradigm is 'This is how things are done'. There follows an incipiently theoretical level (hardly to be included, though, in the category of 'ideas') on which legitimation takes the form of proverbs, moral maxims and traditional wisdom. This type of legitimating lore may be further developed and transmitted in the form of myths, legends, or folk tales. Only then may one come upon explicitly theoretical legitimations, by which specific sectors of the social order are explained and justified by means of specialized bodies of 'knowledge'. Finally, there are the highly theoretical constructions by which the nomos of a society is legitimated *in toto* and in which all less-than-total legitimations are theoretically integrated in an all-embracing *Weltanschauung*. This last level may be described by saying that here the nomos of a society attains theoretical self-consciousness.

There is both an objective and subjective aspect to legitimation. The legitimations exist as objectively valid and available definitions of reality. They are part of the objectivated 'knowledge' of society. If they are to be effective in supporting the social order, however, they will have to be internalized and serve to define subjective reality as well. In other words, effective legitimation implies the establishment of symmetry between objective and subjective definitions of reality. The reality of the world as socially defined must be maintained externally, in the conversation of men with each other, as well as internally, in the way by which the individual apprehends the world within his own consciousness. The essential purpose of all forms of legitimation may thus be described as reality-maintenance, both on the objective and the subjective levels.

It will readily be seen that the area of legitimation is far broader than that of religion, as these two terms have been defined here. Yet there exists an important relationship between the two. It can be described simply by saying that religion has been the historically most widespread and effective instrumentality of legitimation. All legitimation maintains socially defined reality. Religion legitimates so effectively because it relates the precarious reality constructions of empirical societies with ultimate reality. The tenuous realities of the social world are grounded in the sacred *realissimum*, which by definition is beyond the contingencies of human meanings and human activity.

The efficacy of religious legitimation can be brought home by asking an, as it were, recipe question on the construction of worlds. If one imagines oneself as a fully aware founder of a society, a kind of combination of Moses and Machiavelli, one could ask oneself the following question: How can the future continuation of the institutional order, now established *ex nihilo*, be best ensured? There is an obvious answer to the question in terms of power. But let it be assumed that all the means of power have been effectively employed – all opponents have been destroyed, all means of coercion are in one's own hands, reasonably safe provisions have been made for the transmission of power to one's designated successors. There still remains the problem of legitimation, all the more urgent because of the novelty and thus highly conscious precariousness of the new order. The problem would best be solved by applying the following recipe: Let the institutional order be so interpreted as to hide as much as possible, its *constructed* character. Let that which has been stamped out of the ground *ex nihilo* appear as the manifestation of something that has been existent from the beginning of time, or at least from the beginning of this group. Let the people forget that this order was established by men and continues to be dependent upon the consent of men. Let them believe that, in acting out the institutional programmes that have been imposed upon them, they are but realizing the deepest aspirations of their own being and putting themselves in harmony with the fundamental order of the universe. In sum: Set up religious legitimations. There are, of course, wide historical variations in the manner in which this has been done. In one way or another, the basic recipe was followed throughout most of human history. And, actually, the example of the Moses–Machiavelli figuring the whole thing out with cool deliberation may not be as fanciful as all that. There have been very cool minds indeed in the history of religion.

Religion legitimates social institutions by bestowing upon them an ultimately valid ontological status, that is, by *locating* them within a sacred and cosmic frame of reference. The historical constructions of human activity are viewed from a vantage point that, in its own self-definition, transcends both history and man. This can be done in different ways. Probably the most ancient form of this legitimation is the conception of the institutional order as directly reflecting or manifesting the divine structure of the cosmos, that is, the conception of the relationship between society and cosmos as one between microcosm and macrocosm.[3]

Everything 'here below' has its analogue 'up above'. By participating in the institutional order men, *ipso facto*, participate in the divine cosmos. The kinship structure, for example, extends beyond the human realm, with all being (including the being of the gods) conceived of in the structures of kinship as given in the society.[4] Thus there may be not only a totemic 'sociology' but a totemic 'cosmology' as well. The social institutions of kinship then merely reflect the great 'family' of all being, in which the gods participate on a higher level. Human sexuality reflects divine creativity. Every human family reflects the structure of the cosmos, not only in the sense of representing but of embodying it. Or, for another crucial case, the political structure simply extends into the human sphere the power of the divine cosmos. The political authority is conceived of as the agent of the gods, or ideally even as a divine incarnation. Human power, government, and punishment thus become sacramental phenomena, that is, channels by which divine forces are made to impinge upon the lives of men. The ruler speaks for the gods, or *is* a god, and to obey him is to be in a right relationship with the world of the gods.

The microcosm/macrocosm scheme of legitimating the social order, while typical of primitive and archaic societies, has been transformed in the major civilizations.[5] Such transformations are probably inevitable with a certain development of human thought beyond a strictly mythological world view, that is, a world view in which sacred forces are continuously permeating human experience. In the civilizations of eastern Asia the mythological legitimations were transformed into highly abstract philosophical and theological categories, though the essential features of the microcosm/macrocosm scheme remained intact.[6] In China, for instance, even the very rational, virtually secularizing, demythologization of concept of *tao* (the 'right order' or 'right way' of things) permitted the continuing conception of the institutional structure as reflective of cosmic order. In India, on the other hand, the notion of *dharma* (social duty, particularly caste duty) as relating the individual to the universal order of the universe survived most of the radical reinterpretations of the latter's meaning. In Israel the scheme was broken through by the faith in a radically transcendent God of history, and in Greece by the positing of the human soul as the ground for the rational ordering of the world.[7] The latter two transformations had profound consequences for religious legitimation, in the Israelite case leading to the interpretation of institutions in terms of revealed divine imperatives, in the Greek case to interpretations based on rationally conceived assumptions about the nature of man. Both the Israelite and the Greek transformations carried within them the seeds of a secularized view of the social order. The resulting historical developments need not concern us at the moment, nor the fact that large masses of people continue to conceive of society in essentially archaic terms down to our own time and regardless of the transformations in the 'official' definitions of reality. What is important to stress is that, even where the microcosm/macrocosm scheme was broken through, religion continued for many centuries to be the central legitimating agency. Israel legitimated its institutions in terms of the divinely revealed law throughout its existence as an autonomous society.[8] The Greek city, and its subsidiary institutions, continued to be legitimated in religious terms, and these legitimations could even be expanded to apply to the Roman empire in a later era.[9]

To repeat, the historically crucial part of religion in the process of legitimation is explicable in terms of the unique capacity of religion to 'locate' human phenomena within a cosmic frame of reference. All legitimation serves to maintain reality — reality, that is, as defined in a particular human collectivity. Religious legitimation purports to relate the humanly defined reality to ultimate, universal and sacred reality. The inherently precarious and transitory constructions of human activity are thus given the semblance of ultimate security and permanence. Put differently, the humanly constructed nomoi are given a cosmic status.

This cosmization, of course, refers not only to the over-all nomic structures, but to specific institutions and roles within a given society. The cosmic status assigned to these is objectivated, that is, it becomes part of the objectively available reality of the institutions and roles in question. For example, the institution of divine kingship, and the several roles representing it, is apprehended *as* a decisive link between the world of men and the world of the gods. The religious legitimation of power involved in this institution does not appear as an *ex post facto* justification of a few theoreticians, it is objectively present as the institution is encountered by the man in the street in the course of his everyday life. In so far as the man in the street is adequately socialized into the reality of his society he cannot conceive of the king *except as* the bearer of a role that represents the fundamental order of the universe – and, indeed, the same assumption may be made for the king himself. In this manner, the cosmic status of the institution is 'experienced' whenever men come into contact with it in the ordinary course of events.[10]

The 'gains' of this kind of legitimation are readily evident, whether one looks at it from the viewpoint of institutional objectivity or from that of individual subjective consciousness. All institutions possess the character of objectivity and their legitimations, whatever content these may have, must continuously undergird this objectivity. The religious legitimations, however, ground the socially defined reality of the institutions in the ultimate reality of the universe, in reality 'as such'. The institutions are thus given a semblance of inevitability, firmness and durability that is analogous to these qualities as ascribed to the gods themselves. Empirically, institutions are always changing as the exigencies of human activity upon which they are based change. Institutions are always threatened not only by the ravages of time, but by those of conflict and discrepancies between the groups whose activities they are intended to regulate. In terms of the cosmic legitimations, on the other hand, the institutions are magically lifted above these human, historical contingencies. They become inevitable, because they are taken for granted not only by men but by the gods. Their empirical tenuousness is transformed into an overpowering stability as they are understood as but manifestations of the underlying structure of the universe. They transcend the death of individuals and the decay of entire collectivities, because they are now grounded in a sacred time within which merely human history is but an episode. In a sense, then, they become immortal.

Looked at from the viewpoint of individual subjective consciousness, the cosmization of the institutions permits the individual to have an ultimate sense of rightness, both cognitively and normatively, in the roles he is expected to play in society. Human role-playing is always dependent upon the recognition of others. The individual can identify himself with a role only in so far as others have identified him with it. When roles, and the institutions to which they belong, are endowed with cosmic significance, the individual's self-identification with them attains a further dimension. For now it is not only human others who recognize him in the manner appropriate to the role, but those suprahuman others with which the cosmic legitimations populate the universe. His self-identification with the role becomes correspondingly deeper and more stable. He *is* whatever society has identified him as by virtue of a cosmic truth, as it were, and his social being becomes rooted in the sacred reality of the universe. Once more, the transcendence of erosive time is of paramount importance here. An Arabic proverb puts it succinctly: 'Men forget, God remembers'. What men forget, among other things, is their reciprocal identifications in the game of playing society. Social identities and their corresponding roles are assigned to the individual by others, but others are also quite liable to change or withdraw the assignments. They 'forget' who the individual was and, because of the inherent dialectic of recognition and self-recognition, thus powerfully threaten his own recollections of identity. If he can assume that, at any rate, God remembers, his tenuous self-identifications are given a foundation seemingly secure from the shifting reactions of other men. God then becomes the most reliable and ultimately significant other.[11]

Where the microcosm/macrocosm understanding of the relationship between society and cosmos prevails, the parallelism between the two spheres typically extends to specific roles. These are then understood as mimetic reiterations of the cosmic realities for which they are supposed to stand. All social roles are representations of large complexes of objectivated meanings.[12] For example, the role of father represents a wide variety of meanings ascribed to the institution of the family and, more generally, to the institutionalization of sexuality and interpersonal relationships. When this role is legitimated in mimetic terms – the father reiterating 'here below' the actions of creation, sovereignty, or love that have their sacred prototypes 'up above' – then its representative character becomes vastly enhanced. Representation of human meanings becomes mimesis of divine mysteries. Sexual intercourse mimes the creation of the universe. Paternal authority mimes the authority of the gods, paternal solicitude the solicitude of the gods. Like the institutions, then, roles become endowed with a quality of immortality. Also, their objectivity, over and beyond the foibles of the individuals who are their 'temporal' bearers, becomes immensely strengthened. The role of fatherhood confronts the individual as a divinely given facticity, ultimately untouchable not only by his own conceivable transgressions against it but also by all the conceivable vicissitudes of history. The point need hardly be belaboured that legitimation of this kind carries with it extremely powerful and built-in sanctions against individual deviance from the prescribed role performances.

But even where religious legitimation falls short of cosmization and does not permit the transformation of human acts into mimetic representations, it still permits the individual to play his roles with a greater assurance that they are more than ephemeral human productions. At any rate those roles that have been specially circumscribed with religious mandates and sanctions will 'gain' in this way. Even in our own society, for example, where sexuality, the family, and marriage are hardly legitimated in mimetic terms, the roles pertaining to these institutional spheres are effectively maintained by religious legitimations. The contingent formations of a particular historical society, the particular institutions produced out of the polymorphic and pliant material of human sexuality, are legitimated in terms of divine commandment, 'natural law', and sacrament. Even today, then, the role of fatherhood not only has a certain quality of impersonality (that is, detachability from the particular person who performs it – a quality attaching to all social roles), but in its religious legitimation this becomes a quality of suprapersonality by virtue of its relationship to the heavenly father who instituted on earth the order to which the role belongs.

Just as religious legitimation interprets the order of society in terms of an all-embracing, sacred order of the universe, so it relates the disorder that is the antithesis of all socially constructed nomoi to that yawning abyss of chaos that is the oldest antagonist of the sacred. To go against the order of society is always to risk plunging into anomy. To go against the order of society as religiously legitimated, however, is to make a compact with the primeval forces of darkness. To deny reality as it has been socially defined is to risk falling into irreality, because it is well-nigh impossible in the long run to keep up alone and without social support one's own counterdefinitions of the world. When the socially defined reality has come to be identified with the ultimate reality of the universe, then its denial takes on the quality of evil as well as madness. The denier then risks moving into what may be called a negative reality – if one wishes, the reality of the devil. This is well expressed in those archaic mythologies that confront the divine order of the world (such as *tao* in China, *rta* in India, *ma'at* in Egypt) with an underworld or antiworld that has a reality of its own – negative, chaotic, ultimately destructive of all who inhabit it, the realm of demonic monstrosities. As particular religious traditions move away from mythology, this imagery will, of course, change. This happened, for instance, in the highly sophisticated ways in which later Hindu thought developed the original dichotomy of *rta* and *anrta*. But the fundamental confrontation between light and darkness, nomic security and anomic abandonment, remains operative. Thus the violation of one's *dharma* is not just a moral offence against society, but an outrage against the ultimate order that embraces both gods and men and, indeed, all beings.

Men forget. They must, therefore, be reminded over and over again. Indeed, it may be argued that one of the oldest and most important prerequisites for the establishment of culture is the institution of such 'reminders', the terribleness of which for many centuries is perfectly logical in view of the 'forgetfulness' that they were designed to combat.[13] Religious ritual has been a crucial instrument of this process of 'reminding'. Again and again it 'makes present' to those who participate in it the fundamental reality-definitions and their appropriate legitimations. The farther back one goes historically, the more does one find religious ideation (typically in mythological form) embedded in ritual activity – to use more modern terms, theology embedded in worship. A good case can be made that the oldest religious expressions were always ritual in character.[14] The 'action' of a ritual (the Greeks called this its *ergon* or 'work' – from which, incidentally, our word 'orgy' is derived) typically consists of two parts – the things that have to be done (*dromena*) and the things that have to be said (*legoumena*). The performances of the ritual are closely linked to the reiteration of the sacred formulas that 'make present' once more the names and deeds of the gods. Another way of putting this is to say that religious ideation is grounded in religious activity, relating to it in a dialectical manner analogous to the dialectic between human activity and its products discussed earlier in a broader context. Both religious acts and religious legitimations, ritual and mythology, *dromena* and *legoumena, together* serve to 'recall' the traditional meanings embodied in the culture and its major institutions. They restore ever again the continuity between the present moment and the societal tradition, placing the experiences of the individual and the various groups of the society in the context of a history (fictitious or not) that transcends them all. It has been rightly said that society, in its essence, is a memory.[15] It may be added that, through most of human history, this memory has been a religious one.

The dialecticity between religious activity and religious ideation points to another important fact – the rootedness of religion in the practical concerns of everyday life.[16] The religious legitimations, or at least most of them, make little sense if one conceives of them as productions of theoreticians that are then applied *ex post facto* to particular complexes of activity. The need for legitimation arises in the course of activity. Typically, this is in the consciousness of the actors before that of the theoreticians. And, of course, while all members of a society are actors within it, only very few are theoreticians (mystagogues, theologians, and the like). The degree of theoretical elaboration of the religious legitimations will vary with a large number of historical factors, but it would lead to grave misunderstanding if only the more sophisticated legitimations were taken into consideration. To put it simply, most men in history have felt the need for religious legitimation – only very few have been interested in the development of religious 'ideas'.

This does *not* mean, however, that where there exists more complex religious ideation it is to be understood as nothing but a 'reflection' (that is, a dependent variable) of the everyday, practical interests from which it derives. The term 'dialectic' is useful precisely in avoiding this misinterpretation. Religious legitimations arise from human activity, but once crystallized into complexes of meaning that become part of a religious tradition they can attain a measure of autonomy as against this activity. Indeed, they may then *act back upon* actions in everyday life, transforming the latter, sometimes radically. It is probable that this autonomy from practical concerns increases with the degree of theoretical sophistication. For example, the thought of a tribal shaman is likely to be more directly linked to the practical concerns of society than the thought of a professor of systematic theology. In any case, one cannot properly assume *a priori* that to understand the social roots of a particular religious idea is *ipso facto* to understand its later meaning or to be able to predict its later social consequences. 'Intellectuals' (religious or otherwise) sometimes spin out very strange ideas – and very strange ideas sometimes have important historical effects.

Religion thus serves to maintain the reality of that socially constructed world within which men exist in their everyday lives. Its legitimating power, however, has another important dimension – the integration into a comprehensive nomos of precisely those marginal situations in which the reality of everyday life is put in question.[17] It would be erroneous to think of these situations as being rare. On the contrary, every individual passes through such a situation every twenty hours or so – in the experience of sleep and, very importantly, in the transition stages between sleep and wakefulness. In the world of dreams the reality of everyday life is definitely left behind. In the transition stages of falling asleep and waking up again the contours of everyday reality are, at the least, less firm than in the state of fully awake consciousness. The reality of everyday life, therefore, is continuously surrounded by a penumbra of vastly different realities. These, to be sure, are segregated in consciousness as having a special cognitive status (in the consciousness of modern man, a lesser one) and thus generally prevented from massively threatening the primary reality of fully awake existence. Even then, however, the 'dikes' of everyday reality are not always impermeable to the invasion of those other realities that insinuate themselves into consciousness during sleep. There are always the 'nightmares' that continue to haunt in the daytime – specifically, with the 'nightmarish' thought that daytime reality may not be what it purports to be, that behind it lurks a totally different reality that may have as much validity, that indeed world and self may ultimately be something quite different from what they are defined to be by the society in which one lives one's daytime existence. Throughout the greater part of human history these other realities of the nightside of consciousness were taken quite seriously *as* realities, albeit of a different kind. Religion served to integrate these realities with the reality of everyday life, sometimes (in contrast to our modern approach) by ascribing to them a *higher* cognitive status. Dreams and nocturnal visions were related to everyday life in a variety of ways – as warnings, prophecies, or decisive encounters with the sacred, having specific consequences for everyday conduct in society. Within a modern ('scientific') frame of reference, of course, religion is less capable of performing this integration. Other legitimating conceptualizations, such as those of modern psychology, have taken the place of religion. All the same, where religion continues to be meaningful as an interpretation of existence, its definitions of reality must somehow be able to account for the fact that there are different spheres of reality in the ongoing experience of every-one.[18]

Marginal situations are characterized by the experience of 'ec-stasy' (in the literal sense of *ek-stasis* – standing, or stepping, *outside* reality as commonly defined). The world of dreams is ecstatic with regard to the world of everyday life, and the latter can only retain its primary status in consciousness if some way is found of legitimating the ecstasies within a frame of reference that includes *both* reality spheres. Other bodily states also pro-duce ecstasies of a similar kind, particularly those arising from disease and acute emotional disturbance. The confrontation with death (be it through actually witnessing the death of others or anticipating one's own death in the imagination) constitutes what is probably the most important marginal situation.[19] Death rad-ically challenges *all* socially objectivated definitions of reality – of the world, of others, and of self. Death radically puts in question the taken-for-granted, 'business-as-usual' attitude in which one exists in everyday life. Here, everything in the daytime world of existence in society is massively threatened with 'irreality' – that is, everything in that world becomes dubious, eventually unreal, other than one had used to think. In so far as the knowledge of death cannot be avoided in any society, legitimations of the re-ality of the social world *in the face of death* are decisive re-quirements in any society. The importance of religion in such legitimations is obvious.

Religion, then, maintains the socially defined reality by legit-imating marginal situations in terms of an all-encompassing sacred reality. This permits the individual who goes through these situations to continue to exist in the world of his society – not 'as if nothing had happened', which is psychologically difficult in the more extreme marginal situations, but in the 'knowledge' that even these events or experiences have a place within a universe that makes sense. It is thus even possible to have 'a good death', that is, to die while retaining to the end a meaningful relationship with the nomos of one's society – subjectively meaningful to oneself and objectively meaningful in the minds of others.

While the ecstasy of marginal situations is a phenomenon of

individual experience, entire societies or social groups may, in times of crisis, undergo such a situation collectively. In other words, there are events affecting entire societies or social groups that provide massive threats to the reality previously taken for granted. Such situations may occur as the result of natural catastrophe, war, or social upheaval. At such times religious legitimations almost invariably come to the front. Furthermore, whenever a society must motivate its members to kill or to risk their lives, thus consenting to being placed in extreme marginal situations, religious legitimations become important. Thus the 'official' exercise of violence, be it in war or in the administration of capital punishment, is almost invariably accompanied by religious symbolizations. In these cases religious legitimation has the already discussed 'gain' of allowing the individual to differentiate between his 'real self' (which is afraid or has scruples) and his self *qua* role-carrier (warrior, hangman, and what not, in which roles he may act the hero, the merciless avenger, and so on). Killing under the auspices of the legitimate authorities has, for this reason, been accompanied from ancient times to today by religious paraphernalia and ritualism. Men go to war and men are put to death amid prayers, blessings, and incantations. The ecstasies of fear and violence are, by these means, kept within the bounds of 'sanity', that is, of the reality of the social world.

To return once more to the dialectic between religious activity and religious ideation, there is a further aspect of this that is extremely important for the reality-maintaining task of religion. This aspect refers to the social-structural prerequisites of any religious (or, for that matter, any other) reality-maintaining process. This may be formulated as follows: Worlds are socially constructed and socially maintained. Their continuing reality, both objective (as common, taken-for-granted facticity) and subjective (as facticity imposing itself on individual consciousness), depends upon *specific* social processes, namely those processes that ongoingly reconstruct and maintain the particular worlds in question. Conversely, the interruption of these social processes threatens the (objective and subjective) reality of the worlds in question. Thus each world requires a social 'base' for its continuing existence as a world that is real to actual human beings. This 'base' may be called its plausibility structure.[20]

This prerequisite applies both to legitimations and to the worlds or nomoi that are legitimated. And, of course, it applies regardless of the fact whether these are religious in quality or not. In the context of the present argument, however, it will be useful to concentrate on examples of religiously legitimated worlds. Thus, for example, the religious world of pre-Columbian Peru was objectively and subjectively real as long as its plausibility structure, namely, pre-Columbian Inca society, remained intact. Objectively, the religious legitimations were ongoingly confirmed in the collective activity taking place within the framework of this world. Subjectively, they were real to the individual whose life was embedded in the same collective activity (leaving aside here the question of the 'unadjusted' Peruvian). Conversely, when the conquering Spaniards destroyed this plausibility structure, the reality of the world based on it began to disintegrate with terrifying rapidity. Whatever may have been his own intentions, when Pizarro killed Atahualpa, he began the destruction of a world of which the Inca was not only the representative but the essential mainstay. By his act, he shattered a world, redefined reality, and consequently redefined the existence of those who had been 'inhabitants' of this world. What previously had been existence in the nomos of the Inca world, now became, first, unspeakable anomy, then a more or less nomized existence on the fringes of the Spaniards' world – that other world, alien and vastly powerful, which imposed itself as reality-defining facticity upon the numbed consciousness of the conquered. Much of the history of Peru, and of Latin America generally, since then has been concerned with the consequences of this world-shattering catastrophe.

These considerations have far-reaching implications for both the sociology and the psychology of religion. There have been religious traditions that have strongly emphasized the necessity of the religious community – such as the Christian *koinonia*, the Muslim *'umma*, the Buddhist *sangha*. These traditions pose particular sociological and psychological problems, and it would be mistaken to reduce them all to abstract common denominators. Nevertheless, it can be said that *all* religious traditions, irrespective of their several 'ecclesiologies' or lack of same, require specific communities for their continuing plausibility. In this sense, the maxim *extra ecclesiam nulla salus* has general empirical applicability, provided one understands *salus* in a theologically rather unpalatable sense – to wit, as continuing plausibility. The reality of the Christian world depends upon the presence of social structures within which this reality is taken for granted and within which successive generations of individuals are socialized in such a way that this world will be real *to them*. When this plausibility structure loses its intactness or continuity, the Christian world begins to totter and its reality ceases to impose itself as self-evident truth. This is the case with the individual – the Crusader, say, who has been captured and is forced to live in a Muslim ambience. It is also the case with large collectivities – as the entire history of Western Christendom since the Middle Ages demonstrates with impressive clarity. In this respect, despite the historical peculiarities of the Christian community, the Christian is subject to the same social-psychological dialectic as the Muslim, the Buddhist, or the Peruvian Indian. A failure to understand this is likely to produce blindness with respect to very important historical developments in all these traditions.

The prerequisite of plausibility structures pertains to entire religious worlds as well as to the legitimations designed to maintain these, but a further differentiation may be made. The firmer the plausibility structure is, the firmer will be the world that is 'based' upon it. In the limiting case (an empirically unavailable one) this will mean that the world, as it were, posits itself and requires no further legitimation beyond its sheer presence. This is a most unlikely case, if only because the socialization of every new generation into the world in question will require legitimation of some sort – children *will* ask 'why'. An empirically more relevant corollary follows, though: The less firm the plausibility structure becomes, the more acute will be the need for world-maintaining legitimations. Typically, therefore, the development of complex legitimations takes place in situations in which plausibility structures are threatened in one way or another. For example, the mutual threat of Christendom and Islam in the Middle Ages required the theoreticians of *both* socio-religious worlds to produce legitimations that vindicated one's own world against the opposing one (and which, typically, also included an 'explanation' of the other world in terms of one's own). This example is particularly instructive because the antagonistic theoreticians employed an essentially similar intellectual apparatus for their contradictory purposes.[21]

It must be stressed very strongly that what is being said here does *not* imply a sociologically deterministic theory of religion. It is *not* implied that any particular religious system is nothing but the effect or 'reflection' of social processes. Rather, the point is that the *same* human activity that produces society also produces religion, with the relation between the two products always being a dialectical one. Thus it is just as possible that, in a particular historical development, a social process is the effect of religious ideation, while in another development the reverse may be the case. The implication of the rootage of religion in human activity is *not* that religion is always a dependent variable in the history of a society, but rather that it derives its objective and subjective reality from human beings, who produce and reproduce it in their ongoing lives. This, however, poses a problem of 'social engineering' for anyone who wishes to maintain the reality of a particular religious system, for to maintain his religion he must maintain (or, if necessary, fabricate) an appropriate plausibility structure. The practical difficulties involved in this will, of course, vary historically.

A theoretically important variation is between situations in which an entire society serves as the plausibility structure for a religious world and situations in which only a subsociety serves as such.[22] In other words, the 'social-engineering' problem differs as between religious monopolies and religious groups seeking to maintain themselves in a situation of pluralistic competition. It is not difficult to see that the problem of world-maintenance is less difficult of solution in the former instance. When an entire society serves as the plausibility structure for a religiously legitimated world, all the important social processes within it serve to confirm and reconfirm the reality of this world. This is so even when the world in question is threatened *from the outside*, as was the case in the Christian–Muslim confrontation during the Middle Ages. The 'social-engineering' problem in such a situation, apart from providing the necessary institutional context for socialization and resocialization under 'correct' auspices (given, in the two instances, in the religious monopolies in education, scholarship, and law), involves the protection of the territorial limits of each plausibility structure (the military frontier between the two worlds being a cognitive frontier as well), their extension if feasible (through Crusades and Holy Wars) and the upkeep of effective controls over dangerous or potentially dangerous deviants within the respective territories. The last can be achieved in different ways, the typical ones being physical destruction of deviant individuals or groups (the favoured Christian way, as in the liquidation of individual heretics by the Inquisition and that of heretical subcommunities along the lines of the Crusade against the Albigensians), and physical segregation of these individuals or groups in such a way that they are kept from significant contact with the 'inhabitants' of the 'correct' world (the favoured Muslim way, as expressed in the Quranic provisions for non-Muslim 'peoples of the book' and the *millet* system that grew out of these, though Christendom used a similar method in dealing with the Jews in its midst). As long as the particular religious system can maintain its monopoly on a society-wide basis, that is, as long as it can continue to utilize the entire society as its plausibility structure, these ways of solving the problem have a high chance of success.

The situation, of course, changes drastically when different religious systems, and their respective institutional 'carriers', are in pluralistic competition with each other. For a while, the old methods of extermination (as in the wars of religion in post-Reformation Europe) and segregation (as in the 'territorial formula' of the Peace of Westphalia that ended the most violent of these wars) may be tried. But it may become quite difficult to either kill off or quarantine the deviant worlds. The problem of 'social engineering' is then transformed into one of constructing and maintaining subsocieties that may serve as plausibility structures for the demonopolized religious systems. This problem will be taken up again in greater detail in a later part of this book. Suffice it to say at this point that such subsocietal plausibility structures typically have a 'sectarian' character, which in itself creates practical as well as theoretical difficulties for the religious groups in question, especially those that retain the institutional and intellectual habits deriving from the happy days when they were monopolies.

For the individual, existing in a particular religious world implies existing in the particular social context within which that world can retain its plausibility. Where the nomos of individual life is more or less co-extensive with that religious world, separation from the latter implies the threat of anomy. Thus travel in areas where there were no Jewish communities was not only ritually impossible but inherently anomic (that is, threatening an anomic disintegration of the only conceivable 'correct' way of living) for the traditional Jew, as travel outside India was for the traditional Hindu. Such journeys into darkness were to be shunned not only because the company of pork-eaters or cow-defilers caused ritual impurity but, more importantly, because their company threatened the 'purity' of the Jewish or Hindu world — that is, its subjective reality or plausibility. Thus the agonizing question of the Babylonian exiles, 'How can one worship Yahweh in an alien land?', has a decisive cognitive dimension, which indeed has been *the* decisive question for diaspora Judaism ever since. Since every religious world is 'based' on a plausibility structure that is itself the product of human activity, every religious world is inherently precarious in its reality. In other words, 'conversion' (that is, individual 'transference' into another world) is always possible in principle. This possibility increases with the degree of instability or discontinuity of the plausibility structure in question. Thus the Jew whose social ambience was limited by the confines of the ghetto was much less conversion-prone than the Jew existing in the 'open societies' of modern Western countries (conversion here referring to 'emigrations' from traditional Judaism to any one of the various worlds 'available' in such societies, not necessarily to conversion to Christianity). Both the theoretical measures of conversion-prevention ('apologetics' in all its forms) and their practical correlates (various procedures of 'maintenance engineering' – development of subsocietal institutions of 'defence', education, and sociability, voluntary restrictions on social contacts that are dangerous to reality-maintenance, voluntary group endogamy, and so on) increase in complexity in such situations. Conversely, the individual who wishes to convert, and (more importantly) to 'stay converted', must engineer his social life in accordance with this purpose. Thus he must dissociate himself from those individuals or groups that constituted the plausibility structure of his past religious reality, and associate himself all the more intensively and (if possible) exclusively with those who serve to maintain his new one. Put succinctly, migration between religious worlds implies migration between their respective plausibility structures.[23] This fact is as relevant for those who wish to foster such migrations as for those wishing to prevent them. In other words, the same social-psychological problem is involved in evangelism and in the 'care of souls'.

The sociology of religion has been able to show in numerous instances the intimate relationship between religion and social solidarity. It is well at this point of the argument to recall the definition of religion used a little earlier – the establishment, through human activity, of an all-embracing sacred order, that is, of a sacred cosmos that will be capable of maintaining itself in the ever-present face of chaos. Every human society, however legitimated, must maintain its solidarity in the face of chaos. Religiously legitimated solidarity brings this fundamental sociological fact into sharper focus. The world of sacred order, by virtue of being an ongoing human production, is ongoingly confronted with the disordering forces of human existence in time. The precariousness of every such world is revealed each time men forget or doubt the reality-defining affirmations, each time they dream reality-denying dreams of 'madness', and most importantly, each time they consciously encounter death. Every human society is, in the last resort, men banded together in the face of death. The power of religion depends, in the last resort, upon the credibility of the banners it puts in the hands of men as they stand before death, or more accurately, as they walk, inevitably towards it.

The Problem of Theodicy

Every nomos is established, over and over again, against the threat of its destruction by the anomic forces endemic to the human condition. In religious terms, the sacred order of the cosmos is reaffirmed, over and over again, in the face of chaos. It is evident that this fact poses a problem on the level of human activity in society, in as much as this activity must be so institutionalized as to continue despite the recurrent intrusion into individual and collective experience of the anomic (or, if one prefers, denomizing) phenomena of suffering, evil and, above all, death. However, a problem is also posed on the level of legitimation. The anomic phenomena must not only be lived through, they must also be explained – to wit, explained in terms of the nomos established in the society in question. An explanation of these phenomena in terms of religious legitimations, of whatever degree of theoretical sophistication, may be called a theodicy.[1]

It is important to stress here particularly (although the same point has already been made generally with respect to religious legitimations) that such an explanation need not entail a complex theoretical system. The illiterate peasant who comments upon the death of a child by referring to the will of God is engaging in theodicy as much as the learned theologian who writes a treatise to demonstrate that the suffering of the innocent does not negate the conception of a God both all-good and all-powerful. All the same, it is possible to differentiate theodicies in terms of their degree of rationality, that is the degree to which they entail a theory that coherently and consistently explains the phenomena in question in terms of an over-all view of the universe.[2] Such a theory, of course, once it is socially established, may be refracted on different levels of sophistication throughout the society. Thus the peasant, when he speaks about the will of God, may himself intend, however inarticulately, the majestic theodicy constructed by the theologian.

There is, however, a basic point that must be made before one looks at the various types of theodicy and their degrees of rationality. This is the point that there is a fundamental attitude, in itself quite irrational, that underlies all of them. This attitude is the surrender of self to the ordering power of society. Put differently, every nomos entails a transcendence of individuality and thus, *ipso facto*, implies a theodicy.[3] Every nomos confronts the individual as a meaningful reality that comprehends him and all his experiences. It bestows sense on his life, also on its discrepant and painful aspects. Indeed, as we have tried to show earlier, this is the decisive reason for the establishment of nomoi in the first place. The nomos locates the individual's life in an all-embracing fabric of meanings that, by its very nature, transcends that life. The individual who adequately internalizes these meanings at the same time transcends himself. His birth, the various stages of his biography and, finally, his future death may now be interpreted by him in a manner that transcends the unique place of these phenomena in his experience. The point is made dramatically clear in the case of rites of passage, in primitive as well as more complex societies. Rites of passage, to be sure, include happy as well as unhappy experiences. It is with respect to the latter ones that they involve an implicit theodicy. The social ritual transforms the individual event in a typical case, just as it transforms individual biography into an episode in the history of the society. The individual is seen as being born, living and suffering, and eventually dying, as his ancestors have done before him and his children will do after him. As he accepts and inwardly appropriates this view of the matter he transcends his own individuality as well as the uniqueness, including the unique pain and the unique terrors, of his individual experiences. He sees himself 'corectly', that is, within the coordinates of reality as defined by his society. He is made capable of suffering 'correctly' and, if all goes well, he may eventually have a 'correct' death (or a 'good death', as it used to be called). In other words, he may 'lose himself' in the meaning-giving nomos of his society. In consequence, the pain becomes more tolerable, the terror less overwhelming, as the sheltering canopy of the nomos extends to cover even those experiences that may reduce the individual to howling animality.

This implicit theodicy of all social order, of course, antecedes any legitimations, religious or otherwise. It serves, however, as the indispensable substratum on which later legitimating edifices can be constructed. It also expresses a very basic psychological constellation, without which it is hard to imagine later legitimations to be successful. Theodicy proper, then, as the religious legitimation of anomic phenomena, is rooted in certain crucial characteristics of human sociation as such.

Every society entails a certain denial of the individual self and its needs, anxieties, and problems. One of the key functions of nomoi is the facilitation of this denial in individual consciousness. There is also an intensification of this self-denying surrender to society and its order that is of particular interest in connection with religion. This is the attitude of masochism, that is, the attitude in which the individual reduces himself to an inert and thinglike object *vis-à-vis* his fellow men, singly or in collectivities or in the nomoi established by them.[4] In this attitude, pain itself, physical or mental, serves to ratify the denial of self to the point where it may actually be subjectively pleasurable. Masochism, typically in conjunction with its complementary attitude of sadism, is a recurrent and important element of human interaction in areas ranging from sexual relations to political discipleship. Its key characteristic is the intoxication of surrender to an other – complete, self-denying, even self-destroying. Any pain or suffering inflicted by the other (who, of course, is posited as the sadistic counterpart to the masochistic self – absolutely dominating, self-affirming, and self-sufficient) serves as proof that the surrender has indeed taken place and that its intoxication is real. 'I am nothing – He is everything – and therein lies my ultimate bliss' – in this formula lies the essence of the masochistic attitude. It transforms the self into nothingness, the other into absolute reality. Its ecstasy consists precisely in this double meta-morphosis, which is profoundly liberating in that it seems to cut all at once through the ambiguities and anguish of separate, indi-vidual subjectivity confronting the subjectivities of others. The fact that the masochistic attitude is inherently predestined to failure, because the self cannot be annihilated this side of death and because the other can only be absolutized in illusion, need not concern us here.[5] The important point for our immediate considerations is that masochism, by its radical self-denial, pro-vides the means by which the individual's suffering and even death can be radically transcended, to the point where the indi-vidual not only finds these experiences bearable but even wel-comes them. Man cannot accept aloneness and he cannot accept meaninglessness. The masochistic surrender is an attempt to escape aloneness by absorption in an other, who at the same time is posited as the only and absolute meaning, at least in the instant in which the surrender occurs. Masochism thus constitutes a curious convulsion both of man's sociality and of his need for meaning. Not being able to stand aloneness, man denies his sep-arateness, and not being able to stand meaninglessness, he finds a paradoxical meaning in self-annihilation. 'I am nothing – and therefore nothing can hurt me', or even more sharply: 'I have died – and therefore I shall not die', and then: 'Come, sweet pain; come, sweet death' – these are the formulas of masochistic liberation.[6]

The masochistic attitude originates in concrete relations with individual others. The lover, say, or the master is posited as total power, absolute meaning, that is, as a *realissimum* into which the tenuous realities of one's own subjectivity may be absorbed. The same attitude, however, can be extended to collectivities of others and, finally, to the nomoi represented by these. It can be sweet to suffer pain at the hands of one's lover – but it can also be sweet to be punished by the sovereign authority of the state. Finally, the self-denying submission to the power of the collective nomos can be liberating in the same way. Here, the concrete other of social experience is vastly magnified in the personification of collective order. Thus it may not only be sweet to die for one's country, but it may even be sweet to be killed by one's country – provided, of course, that one has the proper patriotic viewpoint. Needless to add, the same extension of the masochistic attitude may take on a religious character. Now the other of the masochistic confrontation is projected into the immensity of the cosmos, takes on cosmic dimensions of omnipotence and absoluteness, and can all the more plausibly be posited as ultimate reality. The 'I am nothing – He is everything' now becomes enhanced by the empirical unavailability of the other to whom the masochistic surrender is made. After all one of the inherent difficulties of masochism in human relations is that the other may not play the sadistic role to satisfaction. The sadistic fellow man may refuse or forget to be properly all-powerful, or may simply be incapable of pulling off the act. Even if he succeeds in being something of a credible master for a while, he remains vulnerable, limited, mortal – in fact, remains human. The sadistic god is not handicapped by these empirical imperfections. He remains invulnerable, infinite, immortal by definition. The surrender to him is *ipso facto* protected from the contingencies and uncertainties of merely social masochism – for ever.

It will be clear from the above that masochism, whether religious or not in its intended object, is pretheoretical in character and thus prior to the emergence of any specific theodicies. The masochistic attitude, however, continues as an important motif in a number of attempts at theodicies, and in some of these it is directly expressed in the theoretical constructions themselves. It is thus well to keep in mind that the masochistic attitude is one of the persistent factors of irrationality in the problem of theodicy, no matter what degree of rationality may be attained in various efforts to solve the problem theoretically. Put graphically, in contemplating the spectacle of theologians working out, sometimes with astounding dispassion, the formulas designed to explain the suffering of men, we must not forget at least the possible presence, behind the calm mask of the theoretician, of the worshipper voluptuously grovelling in the dust before the god who punishes and destroys in sovereign majesty.

Theodicy directly affects the individual in his concrete life in society. A plausible theodicy (which, of course, requires an appropriate plausibility structure) permits the individual to integrate the anomic experiences of his biography into the socially established nomos and its subjective correlate in his own consciousness. These experiences, however painful they may be, at least make sense now in terms that are both socially and subjectively convincing. It is important to stress that this does not necessarily mean at all that the individual is now happy or even contented as he undergoes such experiences. It is not happiness that theodicy primarily provides, but meaning. And it is probable (even leaving aside the recurring appearance of the masochistic motif) that, in situations of acute suffering, the need for meaning is as strong as or even stronger than the need for happiness.[7] To be sure, the individual suffering from a tormenting illness, say, or from oppression and exploitation at the hands of fellow men, desires relief from these misfortunes. But he equally desires to know *why* these misfortunes have come to him in the first place. If a theodicy answers, in whatever manner, this question of meaning, it serves a most important purpose for the suffering individual, even if it does not involve a promise that the eventual outcome of his suffering is happiness in this world or the next. It would, for this reason, be misleading to consider theodicies only in terms of their 'redemptive' potential. Indeed, some theodicies carry no promise of 'redemption' at all – except for the redeeming assurance of meaning itself.[8]

The 'gains' of theodicy for society are to be understood in a way analogous to those for the individual. Entire collectivities are thus permitted to integrate anomic events, acute or chronic, into the nomos established in their society. These events are now given 'a place' in the scheme of things, which consequently is protected from the threat of chaotic disintegration that is always implicit in such events. These events are both natural and social in origin. It is not only natural disaster, illness, and death that must be explained in nomic terms, but also the misfortunes that men inflict on one another in the course of their social interaction. Such misfortunes may be acute and critical, or they may be part and parcel of the institutionalized routines of society. 'Why does

God permit the foreigners to conquer us?' 'Why does God permit some men to eat and others to go hungry?' – both these questions are amenable to answers within specific theodicies. One of the very important social functions of theodicies is, indeed, their explanation of the socially prevailing inequalities of power and privilege. In this function, of course, theodicies directly legitimate the particular institutional order in question. It is important to stress in this connection that such theodicies may serve as legitimations *both* for the powerful *and* the powerless, for the privileged *and* for the deprived. For the latter, of course, they may serve as 'opiates' to make their situation less intolerable, and by the same token to prevent them from rebelling against it. For the former, however, they may serve as subjectively quite important justifications of their enjoyment of the power and privilege of their social position. Put simply, theodicies provide the poor with a meaning for their poverty, but may also provide the rich with a meaning for their wealth.[9] In both cases, the result is one of world-maintenance and, very concretely, of the maintenance of the particular institutional order. It is, of course, another question whether the *same* theodicy can serve both groups in this way. If so, the theodicy constitutes an essentially sado-masochistic collusion, on the level of meaning, between oppressors and victims – a phenomenon that is far from rare in history. In other cases, there may be two discrete theodicies established in the society – a theodicy of suffering for one group and a theodicy of happiness for the other.[10] These two theodicies may relate to each other in different ways, that is, with different degrees of 'symmetry'. In all cases, the disintegration of the plausibility of theodices legitimating social inequalities is potentially revolutionary in its consequences, a point that we shall consider further a little later.

It is possible to analyse historical types of theodicies on a continuum of rationality-irrationality.[11] Each type represents a specific posture, in theory and practice, *vis-à-vis* the anomic phenomena to be legitimated or nomized. Needless to say, no attempt can be made here to elaborate an exhaustive typology. It will be useful, however, to look more closely at some of the historically more important types, particularly at those that have had a direct bearing on the history of Western societies.

On the irrational pole of this typological continuum there is the simple, theoretically unelaborated transcendence of self brought about by complete identification with the collectivity.[12] This may but need not be masochistic in character. What is essential here is that there is no conception of the individual as sharply distinct from his collectivity. The individual's innermost being is considered to be the fact of his belonging to the collectivity – the clan, the tribe, the nation, or what not. This identification of the individual with all others with whom he significantly interacts makes for a merging of his being with theirs, both in happiness and in misfortune. The identification is typically apprehended as being congenital and thus inevitable for the individual. It is carried in his blood, and he cannot deny it unless he denies his own being. This leads to the consequence that the individual's own biographical misfortunes, including the final misfortune of having to die, are weakened at least in their anomic impact by being apprehended as only episodes in the continuing history of the collectivity with which the individual is identified. The stronger this identification, the weaker will be the threat of anomy arising from the misfortunes of individual biography.[13] To be sure, there still remains a problem of legitimating certain collective misfortunes, such as epidemics, or famines, or foreign conquests, and specific theodicies may be established for this purpose. This task is, however, made easier by the identification of the individual with his collectivity for a very simple reason: The individual's mortality is empirically available, that of the collectivity, typically, is not. The individual knows that he will die and, consequently, that some of his misfortunes can never be alleviated within his lifetime. If he loses a limb, for instance, it can never be restored to him. The collectivity, on the other hand, can usually be conceived of as immortal. It may suffer misfortunes, but these can be interpreted as only transitory episodes in its over-all history. Thus the individual dying on the battlefield at the hands of the foreign conqueror may not look forward to his own resurrection or immortality, but he can do so with regard to his group. To the extent that he subjectively identifies himself with that group, his death will have meaning for him even if it is unembellished with any 'individualized' legitimations. Such identification, therefore, posits an implicit theodicy, without the need for further theoretical rationalization.

The prototype of this kind of implicit theodicy may be found in primitive religion.[14] In the latter, there is typically not only a continuity between individual and collectivity, but also between society and nature. The life of the individual is embedded in the life of the collectivity, as the latter is in turn embedded in the totality of being, human as well as non-human. The entire universe is pervaded by the same sacred forces, from *mana* in its original prepersonal form to the later animistic and mythological personifications. Thus the life of men is not sharply separated from the life that extends throughout the universe. As long as they remain within the socially established nomos, they participate in a universal being that also assigns 'a place' to the phenomena of pain and death. The cross-cultural frequency of fertility ritualism is one of the best illustrations of this.[15] The same sacred forces that produce the rhythms of nature are apprehended as pulsating through men's bodies and souls, especially expressing themselves in their sexuality. If men, then, are in tune with the rhythms of these forces within their own being, they are *ipso facto* in tune with the fundamental order of all being – an order that, by definition, includes and thus legitimates the cycles of birth, decay, death, and regeneration. Consequently, the decay and death of the individual is legitimated by means of its 'placement' within the larger order of cosmic cycles. The fertility rituals (and, *mutatis mutandis*, the funerary rituals) reaffirm this legitimation over and over again, with each reaffirmation positing an, as it were, *ad hoc* theodicy. It is important to see that such a theodicy need not necessarily include any hope for an individual after-life or immortality. Not only the individual's body but also his soul (if such is assumed) may disintegrate and perish – what remains, as the ultimately meaning-giving fact, is the eternal eurhythmy of the cosmos. Men and animals, as individuals and in

groups, participate in this and, by surrendering to it, can trans-
pose their suffering and their deaths to a plane of inherently
comforting cosmic meaning.

More specifically, such primitive theodicies typically posit an
ontological continuity between the generations.[16] The individual finds his ancestors continuing mysteriously within himself, and in the same way he projects his own being into his
children and later descendants. As a result, he acquires a (to him)
quite concrete immortality, which drastically relativizes the mortality as well as the lesser misfortunes of his empirical biography.
'I must die – but my children and children's children will live on
for ever' – this is the typical formula for this kind of theodicy.
The entire collectivity, bound together by ties of blood, thus
becomes (to its own self-understanding) quite concretely immortal, for it carries with it through time the *same* fundamental life
that is incarnate in each of its members. To destroy this immortality, an enemy must eradicate every last living soul belonging to
the collectivity – a far from uncommon practice in history, it
may be added. The same participation of all in the life of all,
furthermore, legitimates whatever social inequalities may exist
within the collectivity. The power and privilege held by the few
is held, as it were, vicariously for the many, who participate in it
by virtue of this identification with the collective totality. The
chief, say, may possess a dozen wives while the commoner may
only have one, but for the latter to be resentful of this would be as
foolish as for a lesser limb to be jealous of the head. In all these
cases, there may be added a masochistic element, in so far as the
suffering inflicted by the sacred forces or their human representatives may be directly welcomed as empirical proof of one's
participation in the meaning-giving scheme of things.

Theodicy by self-transcending participation is not limited to
primitive religions. It typically continues, albeit in theoretically
more refined forms, wherever the microcosm/macrocosm
scheme prevails.[17] For example, the Chinese peasant could die
calmly in the assurance that he would live on in his descendants
as his ancestors have lived on in him, but the Confucian gentle-
man could have the same assurance legitimated further by refer-

ence to the fundamental *tao* with which his life and his dying were properly attuned. One may add that, generally, a similar *ad hoc* theodicy is operative whenever men fully identify with a particular collectivity and its nomos, on whatever level of theoretical sophistication. The primitive prototype thus continues historically in a variety of more or less complex modifications.

One historically important religious phenomenon in which the theodicy of self-transcendent participation appears over and over again is mysticism.[18] It cannot be our purpose here to discuss the innumerable variations in which this phenomenon has recurred in religious history. We can define mysticism, for our present purposes, as the religious attitude in which man seeks union with the sacred forces or beings. In its ideal-type form, mysticism entails the claim that such union has, indeed, empirically taken place – all individuality vanishes and is absorbed in the all-pervasive ocean of divinity. In this form, mysticism provides the afore-mentioned theodicy in a just about perfect manner. The individual's sufferings and death become insignificant trivia, fundamentally unreal as compared with the overwhelming reality of the mystical experience of union, as indeed everything in the mundane life of the individual becomes fundamentally unreal, illusionary, a mirage taken seriously only as long as one's vision is obscured by the 'veil of *maya*'. The same trivialization, of course, extends to the mundane life of others, individually and collectively. Mysticism does not always appear in this perfect form, of course, but even in its modified appearances (modified, that is, in that *total* union with the divine is not attained or sought, for theoretical or practical reasons), it brings about an attitude of surrender that carries with it its own theodicy. Put crudely, to the same extent that everything is or is in God, everything is good – the problem of theodicy is thereby effectively *aufgehoben*, which indeed may be considered the principal theoretical and psychological 'gain' of mysticism. The extent to which the mystical surrender may be called masochistic varies empirically, but it is safe to say that a strong masochistic element is present in nearly all varieties of mysticism, as evidenced by the cross-cultural recurrence of ascetic self-mortification and self-torture in connection with mystical phenomena. Where the perfect union is achieved, the annihilation of the self and its absorption by the divine *realissimum* constitute the highest bliss imaginable, the culmination of the mystical quest in ineffable ecstasy. The following passage from the writings of the Muslim mystic Jalalu'l-Din Rumi may serve as an illustration (others like it could be taken, almost at random, from the world literature of mysticism):

> I died as mineral and became a plant,
> I died as plant and rose to animal,
> I died as animal and I was Man.
> Why should I fear? When was I less by dying?
> Yet once more I shall die as Man, to soar
> With angels blest; but even from angelhood
> I must pass on: *all except God doth perish.*
> When I have sacrificed my angel-soul,
> I shall become what no mind e'er conceived.
> Oh, let me not exist! for Non-existence
> Proclaims in organ tones: *to Him we shall return.*[19]

It goes without saying that mysticism, especially in the context of the great world religions, has given birth to complex theoretical systems, some of which contained explicit theodicies of great rational consistency. The point here is simply that there is a continuation in various mystical traditions of the prototypical theodicy of self-transcendence discussed before, sometimes rationalized in terms of highly sophisticated theories, sometimes in a resurgence of very archaic irrational impulses.

On the other pole of the rational-irrational continuum of theodicies, the most rational one, we find the *karma-samsara* complex, as developed in the religious thought of India.[20] In the ingenious combination of the conceptions of *karma* (the inexorable law of cause and effect ruling all actions, human or otherwise, in the universe) and *samsara* (the wheel of rebirths), every conceivable anomy is integrated within a thoroughly rational, all-embracing interpretation of the universe. Nothing, so to speak, is left out.[21] Every human action has its necessary consequences and every human situation is the necessary consequence of past human actions. Thus the life of the individual is only an ephemeral link in a causal chain that extends infinitely into both past and future. It follows that the individual has no one to blame for his misfortunes except himself – and, conversely, he may ascribe his good fortune to nothing but his own merits. The *karmasamsara* complex thus affords an example of complete symmetry between the theodicies of suffering and of happiness. It legitimates the conditions of all social strata simultaneously and, in its linkage with the conception of *dharma* (social duty, particularly caste duty), constitutes the most thoroughly conservative religious system devised in history. It is not surprising that one princely house after another invited its adoption (practically, the establishment of the caste system by immigrant Brahmins, acting in the capacity of 'social engineers') until it had spread throughout the Indian subcontinent.[22] The Code of Manu (even if we cannot be sure today to what extent its legislation was socially effective or was merely the wishful thinking of its Brahmin authors) gives a good idea of the ideological 'gains' the system provided for its upper strata.

There is a stark harshness about these conceptions that was mitigated in popular Hinduism in a variety of ways – magical practices, devotional and mystical exercises, intercessions with various divinities to intervene in the inexorable processes of *karma-samsara* – and, most basic of all, the simple faith that obedience to one's *dharma* will improve one's lot in future reincarnations. It goes without saying that many, indeed most of these manifestations of popular Hinduism are far from the cold rationality with which the system is formulated in, say, the more theoretical portions of the Upanishads. A certain fortitude of spirit was certainly required to accept the revulsion from being itself as expressed, for example, in the following passage from the Maitri Upanishad:

In this ill-smelling, unsubstantial body, which is a conglomerate of bone, skin, muscle, marrow, flesh, semen, blood, mucus, tears, rheum, faeces, urine, wind, bile, and phlegm, what is the good of enjoyment of desires? . . .
And we see that this whole world is decaying, as these gnats,

mosquitoes, and the like, the grass, and the trees that arise and perish.

But, indeed, what of these? ... Among other things, there is the drying up of great oceans, the falling away of mountain peaks, the deviation of the fixed pole-star, the cutting of the wind-cords [of the stars], the submergence of the earth, the retreat of the celestials from their station.

In this sort of cycle of existence [samsara] what is the good of enjoyment of desires, when after a man has fed on them there is seen repeatedly his return here to earth?[23]

Where the starkness of this vision was rationally pursued to its conclusions, typically an enterprise to which only intellectuals inclined, there followed, not surprisingly, a notion of redemption as final liberation from the endless, horror-filled cycle of rebirths (more aptly called a wheel of deaths than a wheel of life). There were, of course, various versions of this redemption.[24] In the Upanishads itself is found the conception of the *atman-brahman*, the ultimate identity of the individual soul with the divine unity underlying all phenomena in the universe. In the Maitri Upanishad, the same hope for liberation is expressed immediately after the passage just quoted:

Be pleased to deliver me. In this cycle of existence I am like a frog in a waterless well. Sir [Sakayanya, one who knows the true nature of the *Atman*], you are our way of escape – yea, you are our way of escape![25]

In the mystical immersion in the *atman-brahman* (for which there are widely different recipes within Hindu soteriology), the restless movements of being, which are the recurrent source of *karma*, come to a stop. All has become one – motionless, eternal, and without individuality. Here, it may be said, the perfect rationality of the *karma-samsara*, having extended itself to its ultimate limit, overreaches itself and falls back into the irrational prototype of self-transcendent participation characteristic of all mysticism.[26]

Buddhism probably represents the most radical rationalization of the theoretical foundations of the *karma-samsara* complex, on the level of soteriology and that of its concomitant theodicy.[27] As in the case of Hinduism, of course, a sharp difference must be made between the Buddhism of monastic intellectuals, the 'carriers' of the authentic traditions, and the syncretistic Buddhism of the masses. This is important in both of the great historical branches of Buddhism, the Theravada and Mahayana traditions. An admixture of innumerable irrational elements, similar to that already remarked upon in connection with popular Hinduism, is to be found in the mass religiosity of the countries commonly called Buddhist (an appellation that properly ought to be put in quotation marks – though, presumably, no more so than that of Christian as applied to the Western Middle Ages). In original Buddhism, however, particularly as it is embodied in the Pali canon, as well as in most soteriological doctrines of the various intellectual schools, the rationalization of *karma-samsara* attains a degree rarely if ever achieved within the bounds of orthodox Hindu thought. Gods and demons, the whole cosmos of mythology, the multitude of worlds of the Indian religious imagination – all these disappear, not by explicit denial but by being declared irrelevant. What remains is man, who, on the basis of his right understanding of the laws of being (summed up in the 'three universal truths' – *anichcha* or impermanence, *dukkha* or sorrow, *anatta* or non-selfhood), rationally sets out to fashion his own salvation and ultimately to attain it in *nibbana* (or *nirvana*). There is no place here for any religious attitudes except the coolness of rational understanding and rational action to attain the goal of this understanding. In this frame of reference, the problem of theodicy is solved in the most rational manner conceivable, namely by eliminating any and all intermediaries between man and the rational order of the universe. Finally, the problem of theodicy disappears because the anomic phenomena that gave rise to it are revealed to be but fugitive illusions – as, indeed, in the conception of *anatta*, is the individual who posed the problem. We may here leave open the question whether this may not also involve the kind of 'overreaching' of rationality that we referred to earlier in connection with Hindu soteriology.

Between the extreme poles of the rational-irrational continuum there are a variety of theodicy types, capable of various
degrees of theoretical rationalization.[28] A theodicy may, first, be
established by projecting compensation for the anomic phenomena into a future understood in this-worldly terms. When the
proper time comes (typically, as a result of some divine intervention), the sufferers will be consoled and the unjust will be
punished. In other words, the suffering and the injustice of the
present are explained with reference to their future nomization.
Under this category, of course, must be placed the different
manifestations of religious messianism, millenarianism, and eschatology.[29] These manifestations, as one would expect, are historically associated with times of crisis and disaster, naturally or
socially caused. For example, the sufferings of the Black Death
gave birth to a number of violent millenarian movements, but so
did the social displacements brought on by the Industrial Revolution. 'The Lord is coming!' – this has been a rallying cry in
times of acute affliction over and over again. Within the orbit of
the Biblical tradition (that is, the Jewish-Christian-Muslim
orbit), as a result of its pervasive stress on the historical dimension of a divine action, this rallying cry has been particularly
frequent. From the pre-exilic prophets of ancient Israel to the
fantastic figure of Shabbatai Zvi, from the imminent expectation
of the *parousia* in the first Christian communities to the great
millenarian movements of modern Protestantism, from the Ab-
basid rebellion to the Sudanese Mahdi – the cry repeats itself,
with whatever modifications in ideational content. The land is
dry and parched – but soon Yahweh will come forth from his
holy mountain and make the clouds give water. The martyrs are
dying in the arena – but soon Christ will appear on the clouds,
bringing down the Beast and setting up his Kingdom. The
infidels rule the land – but soon will come the Mahdi, assisted by
the resurrected saints of all ages, and establish the universal rule
of Islam. And so on, with the secularized eschatologies of the
modern West standing in the same continuous tradition that,
presumably, has its roots in ancient Israel as far back as the
eighth century BC. With greater modifications, however, the

messianic-millenarian complex can also be found outside the orbit of the Biblical tradition – as, for instance, in such movements as the Taiping Rebellion, the Ghost Dance, or the Cargo Cults.

The messianic-millenarian complex posits a theodicy by relativizing the suffering or injustice of the present in terms of their being overcome in a glorious future. In other words, the anomic phenomena are legitimated by reference to a future nomization, thus reintegrating them within an over-all meaningful order. This theodicy will be rational to the extent that it involves a coherent theory of history (a condition, one may say, that is generally fulfilled in the case of messianic-millenarian movements within the Biblical orbit). It will be actually or potentially revolutionary to the extent that the divine action about to intervene in the course of events requires or allows human cooperation.

This type of theodicy faces an obvious practical difficulty – it is highly vulnerable to empirical disconfirmation. There are, to be sure, various cognitive and psychological mechanisms to rationalize empirical counter-evidence.[30] All the same, there remains a theoretical problem in accounting for the fact that Yahweh has *not* brought the rain, that the *parousia* is delayed longer and longer, that the alleged Mahdi turns out to be but another all too mundane ruler, and so on. This inherent difficulty is typically solved by transposing the theodicy either to another world or to another reality somehow hidden within this one. In either case, it will be immune to empirical disconfirmation. This, as it were, refinement of the messianic-millenarian complex points to a second important type of 'intermediate' theodicies, in which compensation is promised in other-worldly terms.

In its simplest form, this type of theodicy maintains a reversal of present sufferings and evils in a life after death. One is probably on safe ground if one speculates that the need for such a theodicy was very important in the origins of notions concerning immortality. It is no longer enough to look for divine compensation in one's own lifetime or that of one's descendants. One now looks for it beyond the grave. There, at last, the sufferer will be comforted, the good man rewarded, and the wicked punished. In other words, the after-life becomes the locale of nomization. This transposition is probably more likely to the extent that the prototypical theodicy by self-transcendent participation weakens in plausibility, a process related to progressive individuation. It may be observed in a number of discrete religious traditions.[31] For example, ancient Egypt as well as ancient China had notions concerning compensations in an after-life, though these do not necessarily involve judgement on the basis of ethical principles. It will be evident that, unlike the this-worldly theodicy of the messianic-millenarian complex, the other-worldly type of theodicy is more likely to be conservative than revolutionary in its effect.

The same type of theodicy, however, can immunize itself to empirical disconfirmation by more complicated means. Thus redemption may be historically operative, in this world, but in a hidden, empirically unverifiable manner. The reinterpretation of Israelite messianic hopes in terms of the 'suffering servant' idea, by Deutero-Isaiah during the period of the Babylonian exile, is a classical example of such a theodicy. The reinterpretation of the messianic mission of Shabbatai Zvi, after the latter's apostasy to Islam, is a very intriguing example of a similar process in more modern Jewish history. In these cases, the concrete messianic-millenarian hope is retained, but at the same time transposed to a mysterious, empirically inaccessible sphere, in which it is safe from the contingencies of history.[32]

A third 'intermediate' type of theodicies is the dualistic one, which has been especially characteristic of the religious form-ations of ancient Iran.[33] The universe is conceived of as the arena of a struggle between two mighty forces of good and evil. These were personified in Zoroastrianism in the gods Ahura Mazda and Ahriman, though in later developments of Iranian dualism, such as Mithraism and Manichaeism, more abstract conceptions emerged. In these formations, all anomic phenom-ena are, of course, ascribed to the evil or negative forces, while all nomization is understood as the progressive victory of their good or positive antagonist. Man is a participant in the cosmic struggle; redemption (be it in this world or the next) consists of his engagement in the struggle on the 'right' side. It goes without saying that this scheme can manifest itself on quite different levels of theoretical sophistication.

In the history of Western religion the theodicy of dualism was most important in the centuries-long influence of Gnosticism.[34] Here the dualism was understood as one between spirit and matter. This world in its material totality was the creation of negative forces, identified by Christian Gnostics with the divinity of the Old Testament. The good divinity did not create this world, and therefore cannot be held accountable for its imperfections. The anomic phenomena in this world, consequently, are not understood as disturbing intrusions of disorder into an orderly cosmos. On the contrary, this world *is* the realm of disorder, of negativity and chaos, and it is man (or rather, the spirit within man) who is the intruder, the stranger from another realm. Redemption consists in the return of the spirit from its exile in this world to its true home, a realm of light totally other than anything existing within the realities of the material universe. The hope for redemption is thus associated with a profound nostalgia for man's true home, as expressed in the following passage from a Gnostic text:

In that world [of darkness] I dwelt thousands of myriads of years, and nobody knew of me that I was there ... Year upon year and generation upon generation I was there, and they did not know about me that I dwelt in their world.

Or again, from a Manichaean text:

Now, O our gracious Father, numberless myriads of years have passed since we were separated from thee. Thy beloved shining living countenance we long to behold.[35]

Dualistic schemes of this type solve the problem of theodicy by, as it were, transposing its terms. The empirical universe ceases to be a cosmos and becomes either the arena within which cosmization is in the making (as in classical Zoroastrianism) or is actually conceived as the realm of chaos (as in the various Gnostic systems). What appears as anomy is, therefore, that which is quite appropriate to this unfinished or negative realm; nomos is either not yet achieved or is to be sought in realms utterly beyond the realities of the empirical universe. In the development of this type of dualism it followed quite logically that everything associated with this world, notably the physical and historical being of man, was radically devaluated. Matter came to be understood as negative reality, as did the human body and all its works. Empirical history, furthermore, was excluded *a priori* from any redemptive significance. In other words, dualistic theodicies tend to be acosmic, ascetic, and ahistorical. It is not difficult to understand why they posed such a potent threat to the world view of the several traditions derived from Biblical religion, as can be seen in the struggles of 'official' Judaism, Christianity, and Islam with various Gnostic movements arising within them.[36]

It will be evident without much elaboration that the problem of theodicy appears most sharply in radical and ethical monotheism, that is, within the orbit of Biblical religion. If all rival or minor divinities are radically eliminated, and if not only all power but all ethical values are ascribed to the one God who created all things in this or any other world, then the problem of theodicy becomes a pointed question directed to this very conception. Indeed, more than in any other religious constellation, it may be said that this type of monotheism stands or falls with its capacity to solve the question of theodicy, 'How can God permit . . .?'

As we have indicated before, the development of Biblical eschatology from concrete historical expectations to soteriological constructions incapable of empirical disconfirmation is one important aspect of the problem as it was met within the orbit of Biblical religion. There is also, however, another aspect, of particular importance for understanding the development beyond the period of ancient Israel. This aspect is the relationship between Biblical theodicy and the masochistic attitude.

Every religion posits an other confronting man as an objective, powerful reality. The masochistic attitude, as we have tried to show, is one of several basic postures that man can take *vis-à-vis* this other. In the orbit of Biblical religion, however, the masochistic attitude takes on a peculiar character, as a result of the immense tension brought about by the problem of theodicy under these circumstances. It is one thing to surrender in masochistic ecstasy to, say, Shiva in his *avatar* as the cosmic destroyer, Shiva as he performs his great dance of creation on a mountain of human skulls. After all, he is not the only divinity in the Hindu scheme, nor is he burdened with anything approaching the ethical quality attributed to the God of the Bible. Religious masochism takes on a peculiar profile in the Biblical orbit precisely because the problem of theodicy becomes unbearably acute when the other is defined as a totally powerful *and* totally righteous God, creator of both man and universe. It is the voice of this terrible God that must now be so overwhelming as to drown out the cry of protest of tormented man, and, what is more, to convert that cry into a confession of self-abasement *ad maiorem Dei gloriam*. The Biblical God is radically transcendentalized, that is, posited as the totally other (*totaliter aliter*) *vis-à-vis* man. In this transcendentalization there is implicit from the start the masochistic solution *par excellence* to the problem of theodicy – submission to the totally other, who can be neither questioned nor challenged, and who, by his very nature, is sovereignly above any human ethical and generally nomic standards.

The classic *loci* for this submission, of course, are already to be found in the Book of Job. 'Though he slay me, yet will I trust in him', declares Job. And then, after the awesome manifestation of God in the whirlwind, Job confesses his own nothingness before the sovereign power that has been revealed to him: 'Wherefore I abhor myself, and repent in dust and ashes'. In this 'wherefore' lies the pathos and the strange logic of the masochistic attitude. The question of theodicy is asked, passionately and insistently, almost to the point where it becomes an open accusation against God. The question, however, is not answered rationally, as in the various efforts by Job's friends. Instead, the questioner is radically challenged as to his right to pose his question in the first place. In other words, the problem of theodicy is solved by an *argumentum ad hominem* in the most drastic sense – more accurately, an *argumentum contra hominem*. The implicit accusation against God is turned around to become an explicit accusation against man. In this curious reversal the problem of theodicy is made to disappear and in its turn appears a problem of anthropodicy (or *iustificatio*, to use a later Christian term). The question of human sin replaces the question of divine justice. It is in this reversal, and in the peculiar relationship it establishes between theodicy and masochism, that we would see one of the fundamental motifs in the development of Biblical religion.[37]

The Book of Job presents us with the, as it were, pure form of religious masochism *vis-à-vis* the Biblical God. In the development of Biblical religion beyond the Old Testament we find both direct continuities and major modifications of this form. For example, the total surrender to the will of God became the fundamental attitude of Islam and, indeed, gave its name to that grandiose simplification of the Biblical tradition (from the Arabic *'aslama*, to submit). The most radical, but also most consistent, development of this posture is to be found in the various conceptions of divine predestination that developed in all the major branches of the Biblical tradition, though with particular ferocity in Islam and later in Calvinism.[38] The Calvinist glorying in the inexorable counsel of God, who from all eternity has elected a few men for salvation and relegated most men to a destiny in hell, is probably the culmination of the masochistic attitude in the history of religion. This becomes especially clear if one reflects that in early Calvinism it was firmly maintained that nobody could possibly know whether he belonged to the elect or not. It was, therefore, always possible that the God who was fervently worshipped, served with all the rigours of the Calvinist ethic and, in some cases, at the risk of life itself (as under the persecutions by the Catholics), had already condemned the worshipper to damnation from the beginning of time and could not be deflected from this decision by any conceivable effort of the latter. The sovereignty of God and the negation of man both reach a terrifying climax here in a vision of the damned themselves joining in the glorification of that same God who has sentenced them to damnation.

It is not difficult to see that this pure form of the masochistic attitude would be hard to sustain for most people, in the main would only be possible for certain religious 'virtuosi'.[39] Less harsh forms of surrender are more likely to prevail in the religion of the masses. In the development of Biblical monotheism the harshness of Job's solution of the problem of theodicy was rarely sustained for long. In popular piety it was most often mitigated through the hope of compensation in another world. In such a modification the masochistic submission, even its rejoicing in suffering, could still take place. But it is less pure to the degree that it includes a hope of its own transformation in a future life – the punishing God will one day stop his punishing, and his celebration in pain will give way to a happier kind of praise. In more sophisticated circles the harshness was broken through by means of various theological interpretations of suffering. We have already mentioned the conception of the 'suffering servant' in Deutero-Isaiah, continued in the 'sanctification of the Name' (*kiddush-hashem*) through suffering in main-line Judaism and in the various doctrines of redemptive suffering in the Jewish heterodox traditions (as, for instance, in the kabbalistic theosophies of 'exile'). Parallels to this may be found in Christianity as well as in Islam. Even in Calvinism the starkness of submission to the inexorable decree of predestination was soon modified by means of various attempts to achieve certainty of election, be it through putative divine blessings upon one's external activities or through an inner conviction of salvation.[40]

Yet all these 'mitigations' of the masochistic theodicy are of less historical importance as compared with the essential Christian solution of the problem, namely, the one posited in Christology.[41] Indeed, we would argue that, despite every conceivable variation of it in the history of Christianity, this may be called *the* fundamental Christian motif – the figure of the incarnate God as the answer to the problem of theodicy, specifically, to the unbearable tension of this problem brought about by the religious development of the Old Testament. And, however the metaphysics of this incarnation and its relationship to man's redemption may have been formulated in the course of Christian theology, it is crucial that the incarnate God is also the God who suffers. Without this suffering, without the agony of the cross, the incarnation would not provide that solution of the problem of theodicy to which, we would contend, it owes its immense religious potency. This has been well stated by Albert Camus, whose understanding of Christianity may be taken as representative of that of its most insightful modern critics:

> In that Christ had suffered, and had suffered voluntarily, suffering was no longer unjust and all pain was necessary. In one sense, Christianity's bitter intuition and legitimate pessimism concerning human behaviour is based on the assumption that over-all injustice is as satisfying to man as total justice. Only the sacrifice of an innocent god could justify the endless and universal torture of innocence. Only the most abject suffering by God could assuage man's agony. If everything, without exception, in heaven and earth is doomed to pain and suffering, then a strange form of happiness is possible.[42]

It is precisely for reason of this 'gain' for the problem of theodicy that the exact relationship of the suffering to the punishing God had to be formulated in Christological doctrine. Only if *both* the full divinity *and* the full humanity of the incarnate Christ could be simultaneously maintained, could the theodicy provided by the incarnation be fully plausible. *This,* and not some obscure metaphysical speculations, was the driving force of the great Christological controversies in the early Christian church, reaching its culmination in the Nicene condemnation of Arianism.[43] The orthodox Christological formulas, as worked out at Nicaea and at later councils, ensured that the suffering of Christ could indeed be identified as suffering on the part of God himself, while simultaneously being genuine human suffering such as poses the problem of theodicy in the first place.

There is, however, an essential condition for the 'strange form of happiness' that is not explicated in the above quotation. This is precisely the condition that binds the Christian theodicy to its masochistic antecedents, at least within the central orthodox traditions of Christianity (as against, for example, the Gnostic heresies). This condition is the affirmation that, after all, Christ suffered *not* for man's innocence, but for his *sin*. It follows that the prerequisite for man's sharing in the redemptive power of Christ's sacrifice is the *acknowledgement of sin*.[44]

The so-called 'Augustinian' solution to the problem of theodicy is not just the presentation of a suffering divinity. We know that the late Greco-Roman era abounded in such notions. The solution rather depends upon the profoundly masochistic shift from the question about the justice of God to that about the sinfulness of man, a shift that, as we indicated, already occurred in the theodicy of the Old Testament. Again, the problem of theodicy is translated into the problem of anthropodicy. But the harshness of this translation is mitigated by the interposition of the suffering God-man between the two partners in the masochistic dialectics of the Book of Job. Put differently, the stark polarization of sovereignty and submission is softened in the figure of the suffering Christ. God suffers in Christ. But Christ's suffering does not justify God, but man. Through Christ the terrible otherness of the Yahweh of the thunderstorms is mellowed. At the same time, because the contemplation of Christ's suffering deepens the conviction of man's unworthiness, the old masochistic surrender is allowed to repeat itself in a more refined, not to say sophisticated, manner. We would contend that the fundamental religious motorics of Christianity cannot be understood if one does not understand this, and that, furthermore, the plausibility of Christianity (at least in its major orthodox forms) stands or falls with the plausibility of this theodicy.

We shall have occasion later in these considerations to discuss the over-all decline in the plausibility of Christianity. Suffice it to say here that this decline has been accompanied by a steady devaluation of the Christian theodicy. In 1755 an earthquake destroyed most of the city of Lisbon and killed a considerable part of its population. This event, slight as it may seem in comparison with the mass horrors of our own time, was an important event for eighteenth-century thought. It violently raised the problem of theodicy and the validity of its Christian solution in some of the best minds of the period, among them Pope, Voltaire, Goethe, and Kant. The First World War, it seems, still produced a sizeable body of literature, particularly in England, with a similar concern. It is very instructive to note that the immeasurably greater horrors of the Second World War did not have a similar result. In so far as these events (particularly those connected with the Nazi atrocities) raised metaphysical questions, as against ethical or political ones, these were typically anthropological rather than theological in character: 'How could men act this way?' rather than, 'How could God permit this?' Even committed Christian spokesmen seem to have had a certain hesitation in reiterating the traditional Christian formulas on the meaning of such events. Within the remaining orthodox and neo-orthodox camps the classical shift from theodicy to anthropodicy has been repeated a number of times, with even the nightmares of Nazism being taken not as a terrible question about the credibility of the Christian God but as a confirmation of the Christian view of human sin. The general response, however, has been a strange silence on the implications of these events for theodicy, and a concentration instead on the anthropological and politico-ethical questions, on which the Christian spokesmen could hope to speak within a frame of reference shared by their secular contemporaries.

The most important historical consequences of the disintegration of the Christian theodicy in the consciousness of Western man has, of course, been the inauguration of an age of revolution. History and human actions in history have become the dominant instrumentalities by which the nomization of suffering and evil is to be sought. Not submission to the will of God, not hope mediated through the figure of Christ, not expectation of a divinely effected *eschaton* serve any longer to assuage most men's anguish. The social theodicy of Christianity (that is, its legitimation of the inequities of society) has been collapsing along with the over-all plausibility of the Christian theodicy – a point, incidentally, that has been seen much more clearly by the antagonists of Christianity than by the Christians themselves.[45] If the Christian explanation of the world no longer holds, then the Christian legitimation of social order cannot be maintained very long either. To quote Camus once more as representative of this realization, man now 'launches the essential undertaking of rebellion, which is that of replacing the reign of grace by the reign of justice'.[46]

Obviously, it cannot be our purpose here to analyse further this revolutionary transformation of consciousness. We have used the different historical constellations of theodicy discussed above only to indicate, in the broadest outline, how man takes different existential and theoretical postures *vis-à-vis* the anomic aspects of his experience, and how different religious systems relate to this enterprise of nomization. Our purpose has been accomplished if we have indicated the centrality of the problem of theodicy for any religious effort at world-maintenance, and indeed also for any effort at the latter on the basis of a non-religious *Weltanschauung*. The worlds that man constructs are forever threatened by the forces of chaos, finally by the inevitable fact of death. Unless anomy, chaos and death can be integrated within the nomos of human life, this nomos will be incapable of prevailing through the exigencies of both collective history and individual biography.[47] To repeat, every human order is a community in the face of death. Theodicy represents the attempt to make a pact with death. Whatever the fate of any historical religion, or that of religion as such, we can be certain that the necessity of this attempt will persist as long as men die and have to make sense of the fact.

Religion and Alienation

It will be convenient at this point to recall the fundamental dialectic that served as the starting point of these considerations –
the three movements of externalization, objectivation, and
internalization, the sum of which constitutes the phenomenon of
society. Man, because of the peculiar character of his biological
makeup, is compelled to externalize himself. Men, collectively,
externalize themselves in common activity and thereby produce
a human world. This world, including that part of it we call
social structure, attains for them the status of objective reality.
The same world, *as* an objective reality, is internalized in socialization, becoming a constituent part of the subjective consciousness of the socialized individual.

Society, in other words, is a product of collective human
activity. As such, and only as such, it confronts the individual as
an objective reality. This confrontation, however oppressive it
may appear to the individual, requires his ongoing internalization of that with which he is confronted. More simply, it
requires his cooperation, that is, his participation in the collective
activity by which the reality of society is ongoingly constructed.
This does not mean, of course, that he must cooperate in the
specific actions that oppress him. But these actions will be real to
him as elements of *social* reality only to the extent that he par-
ticipates, however reluctantly, in the objective meanings that have
been collectively assigned to them. It is this singular aspect that
decisively distinguishes social reality from the reality of nature.
For example, the individual can be killed by his fellow men in a
manner that, in terms of physical events, may be nearly the same
as if these events resulted from natural occurrences without

human intervention – say, being crushed by a rock. Yet, however close the similarity of the physical events may be, an entirely different meaning attaches to these two possibilities of meeting death by being crushed under a rock. The difference is that between an execution and an accident, that is, between an event *within* the social world and an event in which 'brute' nature impinges upon the social world. The individual may 'cooperate' in the execution in a way in which he never can in the accident – namely, by apprehending it in terms of those objective meanings he shares, albeit unhappily, with his executioners. Thus the victim of an execution can die 'correctly' in a way that would be more difficult for the victim of an accident. The example, of course, is extreme. Its point is simply that society, even when it manifests itself to the individual as extreme oppression, is meaningful in a way that nature is not. This proposition holds *a fortiori* in the innumerable cases where social reality is confronted in more agreeable experiences.

As we have seen earlier, the objectivity of the social world means that the individual apprehends it as a reality external to himself and not readily amenable to his wishes. It is *there*, to be reckoned with *as* reality, to come to terms with as 'hard fact'. The individual may daydream of living in a state of delightful polygamy, but he will be compelled to return to the 'hard fact' of his prosaically monogamous situation. The 'prose' of the matter is the common language and meaning system of his society, vastly more massive in its reality than the fugitive 'poetry' of his solitary fantasies. In other words, institutions are real in as much as they share in the objectivity of the social world. The same holds for roles and, very importantly, for internalized roles. In his daydreams the individual may be a Turkish pasha. In the reality of his everyday life he must play the role of sensible middle-class husband. However, it is not only society, as an external structure, that proscribes the role of pasha. The individual's internal structure of consciousness, as it has been shaped by socialization, itself degrades the role of pasha to the status of fantasy, *ipso facto* a status of *lesser* reality. The individual is *real to himself* as a sensible middle-class husband, *not* as a pasha. It is not our concern here to what extent the individual may nevertheless succeed in *realizing* himself as a pasha. The minimal requirement for such realization, certainly, would be the readiness of some others to play the role of odalisques – a technically difficult matter under conditions of monogamy. What concerns us here is simply the important fact that the social world retains its character of objective reality as it is internalized. It is *there* in consciousness too.

In sum, objectivation implies the production of a real social world, external to the individuals inhabiting it; internalization implies that this same social world will have the status of reality within the consciousness of these individuals. The latter process, however, has an additional feature of great importance – to wit, a *duplication of consciousness,* in terms of its socialized and non-socialized components.[1] Consciousness precedes socialization. What is more, it can never be *totally* socialized – if nothing else, the ongoing consciousness of one's own bodily processes ensures this. Socialization, then, is always partial. A *part* of consciousness is shaped by socialization into the form that becomes the individual's socially recognizable identity. As in all products of internalization, there is a dialectical tension between identity as socially (-objectively) assigned and identity as subjectively appropriated – a point of cardinal importance for social psychology, but of little interest to us at the moment.[2] What is more important for our purposes here is that the duplication of consciousness brought about by the internalization of the social world has the consequence of setting aside, congealing or estranging one part of consciousness as against the rest. Put differently, internalization entails self-objectivation. That is, a part of the self becomes objectivated, not just to others but to itself, as a set of representations of the social world – a 'social self', which is and remains in a state of uneasy accommodation with the non-social self-consciousness upon which it has been imposed.[3] For example, the role of middle-class husband becomes an objective 'presence' within the consciousness of the individual. As such, it *confronts* the rest of that consciousness as itself a 'hard fact', corresponding with greater or lesser symmetry (depending upon the 'success' of socialization in this particular case) to the 'hard fact' of the external institution of middle-class marriage.

In other words, the duplication of consciousness results in an *internal* confrontation between socialized and non-socialized components of self, reiterating within consciousness itself the *external* confrontation between society and the individual. In both cases, the confrontation has a dialectical character, in as much as the two elements in each case do not stand in a mechanistic cause/effect relationship, but rather produce each other reciprocally and continually. Furthermore, the two components of self can now engage in an internal conversation with each other.[4] This conversation, of course, reiterates within consciousness the conversation (more accurately, certain typifications of this conversation) that the individual carries on with external others in his social life. For example, the individual attempting to act out the role of pasha in middle-class society will soon find himself engaged in various (in this case, it may be assumed, disagreeable) conversations with others – his wife, members of his family, functionaries of the law, and so on. These external conversations, however, will be replicated within his own consciousness itself. Quite apart from the fact that, say, the law and its morality are likely to have been internalized in the form of 'voices of conscience', there will be at the least an internal conversation between the socially assigned identity of middle-class husband and the subjectively aspired-to identity of pasha, both of these appearing as crystallized 'presences' within consciousness. Which of the two will be more real to the individual is a question of his 'adjustment' to social reality (or, if one wishes, of his 'mental health') – a matter we can leave to policemen and psychotherapists at this point.

Another way of putting this is to say that man produces 'otherness' both outside and inside himself as a result of his life in society. Man's own works, in so far as they are part of a social world, become part of a reality other than himself. They 'escape' him. But man also 'escapes' himself, in so far as part of himself becomes shaped by socialization. The otherness of the social world and the concrete human beings who are the others of social life are internalized in consciousness. In other words, others and otherness are introjected into consciousness. As a result, it becomes a possibility not only that the social world seems strange to the individual, but that he becomes strange to himself in certain aspects of his socialized self.

It is important to emphasize that *this* estrangement is given in the sociality of man, in other words, that it is anthropologically necessary. There are, however, two ways in which it may proceed – one, in which the strangeness of world and self can be reappropriated (*zurueckgeholt*) by the 'recollection' that both world and self are products of one's own activity – the other, in which such reappropriation is no longer possible, and in which social world and socialized self confront the individual as inexorable facticities analogous to the facticities of nature. The latter process may be called alienation.[5]

Put differently, alienation is the process whereby the dialectical relationship between the individual and his world is lost to consciousness. The individual 'forgets' that this world was and continues to be co-produced by him. Alienated consciousness is undialectical consciousness. The essential difference between the socio-cultural world and the world of nature is obscured – namely, the difference that men have made the first, but not the second.[6] In as much as alienated consciousness is based on this fallacy, it is a false consciousness.[7] Put differently again, alienation is an overextension of the process of objectivation, whereby the human ('living') objectivity of the social world is transformed in consciousness into the non-human ('dead') objectivity of nature. Typically, the representations of human, meaningful activity that constitute the reality of the social world are transformed in consciousness into non-human, meaningless, inert 'things'. That is, they are reified.[8] The social world then ceases to be an open arena in which the individual expands his being in meaningful activity, becomes instead a closed aggregate of reifications divorced from present or future activity. The actual relationship between man and his world is inverted in consciousness. The actor becomes *only* that which is acted upon. The producer is apprehended *only* as product. In this loss of the societal dialectic, activity itself comes to appear as something other – namely, as process, destiny or fate.

Three important points about alienation should be made here. First, it must be stressed that the alienated world, with all its aspects, is a phenomenon of *consciousness*, specifically of false consciousness.[9] It is false precisely because man, even while existing in an alienated world, continues to be the co-producer of this world – through alienating activity, which is and remains *his* activity. Paradoxically, man then produces a world that denies him. In other words, man can never actually *become* a thing-like facticity – he can only *apprehend* himself as such, by falsifying his own experience. Second, it would be quite mistaken to think of alienation as a late development of consciousness, a sort of cognitive fall from grace following upon a paradisical state of non-alienated being.[10] On the contrary, all the evidence indicates that consciousness develops, both phylo- and ontogenetically, from an alienated state to what is, at best, a possibility of de-alienation.[11] Both primitive and infantile consciousness apprehends the socio-cultural world in essentially alienated terms – as facticity, necessity, fate. Only much later in history or in the biography of individuals living in specific historical circumstances does the possibility of grasping the socio-cultural world as a human enterprise make its appearance.[12] In other words, the apprehension of the socio-cultural world as an *opus alienum* everywhere precedes its apprehension as man's *opus proprium*. Third, alienation is an entirely different phenomenon from anomy.[13] On the contrary, the apprehension of the socio-cultural world in alienated terms serves to maintain its nomic structures with particular efficacy, precisely because it seemingly immunizes them against the innumerable contingencies of the human enterprise of world-building. The world as man's *opus proprium* is inherently precarious. The world as an *opus alienum* (of the gods, of nature, of the forces of history, or what not) is seemingly everlasting. This last point, of course, is particularly important in understanding the relationship of religion to both alienation and anomy. With it, we come to our immediate concern here.

As we have already seen, religion has been one of the most effective bulwarks against anomy throughout human history. It is now important to see that this very fact is directly related to the alienating propensity of religion. Religion has been so powerful an agency of nomization precisely because it has also been a powerful, probably the most powerful, agency of alienation. By the same token, and in the exact sense indicated above, religion has been a very important form of false consciousness.[14]

One of the essential qualities of the sacred, as encountered in 'religious experience', is otherness, its manifestation as something *totaliter aliter* as compared to ordinary, profane human life.[15] It is precisely this otherness that lies at the heart of religious awe, of numinous dread, of the adoration of what totally transcends all dimensions of the merely human. It is this otherness, for example, that overwhelms Arjuna in the classic vision of Krishna's divine form in the Bhagavad Gita:

> With many faces and eyes, presenting many wondrous sights, bedecked with many celestial ornaments, armed with many divine uplifted weapons; wearing celestial garlands and vestments, anointed with divine perfumes, all-wonderful, resplendent, boundless, and with faces on all sides.

> If the radiance of a thousand suns were to burst forth at once in the sky, that would be like the splendour of the Mighty One.[16]

And then, in more sinister images:

> Beholding Thy great form, O Mighty Lord, with myriads of mouths and eyes, with myriads of arms and thighs and feet, with myriads of bellies, and with myriads of terrible tusks – the worlds are affrighted, and so am I.

> When I look upon Thy blazing form reaching to the skies and shining in many colours, when I see Thee with Thy mouths opened wide and Thy great eyes glowing bright, my inmost soul trembles in fear, and I find neither courage nor peace, O Vishnu![17]

Examples from other religious traditions could be multiplied almost at random, in our own from the awesome throne vision of Isaiah to William Blake's of the tiger, 'burning bright in the forests of the night', pointing beyond its own 'fearful symmetry' to the divine other behind the phenomena of nature. To be sure, in the more 'sophisticated' developments of religion this terror of the alien mystery in the sacred is modified, mellowed, brought closer to man in a variety of mediations. Even there, however, one will not grasp the religious phenomenon if one does not retain an awareness of the otherness continuing as the hidden essence underneath the more 'graceful' or 'gentle' forms (to use the terms employed by Arjuna, as he implores Krishna to show himself again in the, at least relatively, homely shape of the four-armed Vishnu). The awe and fascination of the totally other remains, even there, a leitmotif of the encounter with the sacred.[18]

If one grants the fundamental religious assumption that an other reality somehow impinges or borders upon the empirical world, then these features of the sacred will be dignified with the status of genuine 'experience'. Needless to say, this assumption cannot be made within a sociological or any other scientific frame of reference. In other words, the ultimate epistemological status of these reports of religious men will have to be rigorously bracketed. 'Other worlds' are not empirically available for the purposes of scientific analysis. Or, more accurately, they are only available as meaning-enclaves within *this* world, the world of human experience in nature and history.[19] As such, they must be analysed as are all other human meanings, that is, as elements of the socially constructed world. Put differently, whatever else the constellations of the sacred may be 'ultimately', empirically they are products of human activity and human signification – that is, they are human projections.[20] Human beings, in the course of their externalization, project their meanings into the universe around them. These projections are objectivated in the common worlds of human societies. The 'objectivity' of religious meanings is *produced* objectivity, that is, religious meanings are objectivated projections. It follows that, in so far as these meanings imply an overwhelming sense of otherness, they may be described as *alienated projections*.

In our previous discussion of religious legitimation, we have already seen in what manner the latter provides a semblance of stability and continuity to the intrinsically tenuous formations of social order. We can now identify more accurately the quality that permits religion to do this – to wit, the quality of its alienating power. The fundamental 'recipe' of religious legitimation is the transformation of human products into supra- or non-human facticities. The humanly made world is explained in terms that deny its human production. The human nomos becomes a divine cosmos, or at any rate a reality that derives its meanings from beyond the human sphere. Without going to the extreme of simply *equating* religion with alienation (which would entail an epistemological assumption inadmissible within a scientific frame of reference), we would contend that the historical part of religion in the world-building and world-maintaining enterprises of man is in large measure due to the alienating power inherent in religion.[21] Religion posits the presence in reality of beings and forces that are alien to the human world. Be this as it may, the assertion, in all its forms, is not amenable to empirical inquiry. What is so amenable, though, is the very strong tendency of religion to alienate the human world in the process. In other words, in positing the alien over against the human, religion tends to alienate the human from itself.

It is in *this* sense (and *not* in the sense of regarding the religious assertion as such as epistemologically invalid) that we feel entitled to associate religion with false consciousness, at any rate in terms of a high statistical frequency in its historical manifestations. Whatever may be the 'ultimate' merits of religious explanations of the universe at large, their empirical tendency has been to falsify man's consciousness of that part of the universe shaped by his own activity, namely, the socio-cultural world. This falsification can also be described as mystification.[22] The socio-cultural world, which is an edifice of human meanings, is overlaid with mysteries posited as non-human in their origins. All human productions are, at least potentially, comprehensible in human terms. The veil of mystification thrown over them by religion prevents such comprehension. The objectivated expressions of the human become dark symbols of the divine. And this alienation is powerful over men precisely because it shelters them from the terrors of anomy.

Religion mystifies institutions by explaining them as *given* over and beyond their empirical existence in the history of a society. For example, marriage (more accurately, kinship) is a fundamental institution because of certain biological preconditions of social life. Every society is faced with the problem of providing for its physical procreation. This has meant, empirically, that every society has worked out more or less restrictive 'programmes' for the sexual activity of its members. The historical variability of these 'programmes', of course, is immense, as even a perfunctory glance at the ethnological evidence will indicate. The problem of legitimation is to explain why the particular arrangement that has developed in a particular society, in whatever sequence of historical accidents, should be faithfully adhered to, even if it is at times annoying or downright painful. One efficient way of solving the problem is to mystify the institution in religious terms. The institution of moiety exogamy in certain Brazilian tribes, say, or that of monogamy in our own society may then be legitimated in terms that effectively mask the empirical contingency of these arrangements. To have sexual relations with a member of one's own moiety in Brazil or with someone else's wife in America can then be sanctioned not only as a contravention of the established mores but as an offence against the divine beings posited as the ultimate guardians of the institutions in question. Now it is not only the condemnation and the violence of fellow men that interpose themselves between lust and its desired end, but the avenging power of an angry divinity. There can be little question but that, given an appropriate plausibility structure, very effective controls are provided by such metaphysical legerdemain. There can also be little question but that this is done by means of an alienation of man from his proper world. In the extreme case, as we have seen earlier, marriage then ceases to be apprehended as a human activity at all and becomes a mimetic reiteration of the *hieros gamos* of the gods. The difference between that and a conception of marriage as a sacrament of the church is more one of degree than of quality.

To take another example, every society is faced with the problem of allocating power among its members and typically develops political institutions in consequence. The legitimation of these institutions has the special task of explaining and justifying the requisite employment of means of physical violence, which employment indeed gives their peculiar 'majesty' to the institutions of political life. Again, the mystification of the empirical character of political arrangements in question transforms this 'majesty' from a human to a more-than-human property. Realistic, empirically grounded apprehension concerning people with the power to chop off heads becomes transformed into numinous awe before the 'dread sovereignty' of those who represent the divine will on earth. If circumstances should then develop that make head-chopping politically expedient, the activity in question can be made to seem as but the empirical result of supra-empirical necessities. *Le Roi le veult* becomes, as it were, an echo of 'Thus says the Lord'. Again, it is easy to see how the 'programmes' of political institutionalization are strengthened in this way – once more, by alienating them from their roots in human activity. In both this and the previous example, it must be strongly emphasized that, when we speak of 'transformation', we do *not* imply a chronological progression from non-alienated to alienated apprehensions of these institutions. On the contrary, the progression, if it takes place at all, moves in the opposite direction. The institutions of sexuality and power *first* appear as thoroughly alienated entities, hovering over everyday social life as manifestations from an 'other' reality. Only much later does the possibility of de-alienation appear. Very frequently this appearance goes together with a disintegration of the plausibility structures that previously maintained these institutions.

Mutatis mutandis, the process of mystification extends to the roles clustered in the institutions in question. In other words, the representation implied in every role is mysteriously endowed with the power to represent suprahuman realities. Thus the husband faithfully channelling his lust in the direction of his lawful spouse not only represents in this reiterated action all other faithful husbands, all other complementary roles (including those of faithful wives) and the institution of marriage as a whole, but he now also represents the prototypical action of connubial sexuality as willed by the gods and, finally, represents the gods themselves. Similarly, the king's executioner, who faithfully chops off the head of the lawfully condemned malefactor, not only represents the institutions of kingship, law, and morality as established in his society, but he represents the divine justice that is posited as underlying these. Once more, the terror of suprahuman mysteries overshadows the concrete, empirical terrors of these proceedings.

It is very important to recall in this connection that roles are not only external patterns of conduct, but are internalized within the consciousness of their performers and constitute an essential element of these individuals' subjective identities. The religious mystification of internalized roles further alienates these, in terms of the duplication of consciousness discussed before, but it also facilitates a further process of falsification that may be described as bad faith.[23]

One way of defining bad faith is to say that it replaces choice with fictitious necessities. In other words, the individual, who in fact has a choice between different courses of action, posits one of these courses as necessary. The particular case of bad faith that interests us here is the one where the individual, faced with the choice of acting or not acting within a certain role 'programme', denies this choice on the basis of his identification with the role in question. For example, the faithful husband may tell himself that he has 'no choice' but to 'programme' his sexual activity in accordance with his marital role, suppressing any lustful alternatives as 'impossibilities'. Under conditions of successful socialization, they may then be 'impossible' in fact – the husband may be impotent if he attempts them. Or again, the faithful executioner may tell himself that he has 'no choice' but to follow the 'programme' of head-chopping, suppressing both the emotional and moral inhibitions (compassion and scruples, say) to this course of action, which he posits as inexorable necessity for himself *qua* executioner.

A different way of saying this is to say that bad faith is that form of false consciousness in which the dialectic between the socialized self and the self in its totality is lost to consciousness.[24] As we have seen before, alienation and false consciousness always entail a severance, in consciousness, of the dialectical relationship between man and his products, that is, a denial of the fundamental socio-cultural dialectic. This dialectic, however, is internalized in socialization. Just as man confronts his world externally, he confronts its internalized presence within his own consciousness. *Both* confrontations are dialectical in character. False consciousness, in consequence, may refer to both the external and the internalized relationship of man to his world. In so far as socialized identity is part of that world, it is possible for man to apprehend it in the same alienated mode, that is, in false consciousness. Whereas in fact there is a dialectic between socialized identity and the total self, false consciousness fully identifies the latter with the former. The duplication of consciousness brought about by socialization, and the concomitant internalization of the socio-cultural dialectic, is thus denied. A false unity of consciousness is posited instead, with the individual identifying himself totally with the internalized roles and the socially assigned identity constituted by them. For example, any relevant expressions of self not channelled in the role of faithful husband are denied. Put differently, the internal conversation between husband and (potential) adulterer is interrupted. The individual sees himself as *nothing but* a husband in those areas of his life to which this role pertains. He has become a husband *tout court*, *the* husband of the institutional *dramatis personae*. Social type and subjective identity have merged in his consciousness. In as much as such typification is alienating, identity has itself become alienated. And in as much as such merging is in fact, anthropologically, impossible, it constitutes a fabrication of false consciousness. The individual acting on this presupposition is acting in bad faith.

It is once more very important not to confuse this phenomenon of subjective alienation with anomy. On the contrary, such alienation can be a most effective barrier against anomy. Once the false unity of the self is established, and as long as it remains

plausible, it is likely to be a source of inner strength. Ambi-
valences are removed. Contingencies become certainties. There
is no more hesitation between alternative possibilities of conduct.
The individual 'knows who he is' – a psychologically most satis-
factory condition. Bad faith in no way presupposes some sort of
inner turmoil or 'bad conscience'. On the contrary, the individual who seeks to divest himself of the bad faith institutionalized in his situation in society is likely to suffer
psychologically and in his 'conscience', quite apart from the external difficulties he will probably encounter as a result of such
'unprogrammed' ventures.

It will be clear from the above that bad faith, just as false
consciousness in general, can occur without its being legitimated
religiously. We would also emphasize very strongly that religion
need not necessarily entail bad faith. But it will be seen without
difficulty, if the previous argument is granted, that religion can
be a powerful instrument for the effective maintenance of bad
faith. Just as religion mystifies and thus fortifies the illusionary
autonomy of the humanly produced world, so it mystifies and
fortifies its introjection in individual consciousness. The
internalized roles carry with them the mysterious power ascribed
to them by their religious legitimations. Socialized identity as a
whole can then be apprehended by the individual as something
sacred, grounded in the 'nature of things' as created or willed by
the gods. As such, it loses its character as a product of human
activity. It becomes an inevitable *datum*. Its reality is directly
grounded in the suprahuman *realissimum* posited by religion.
The individual is now not only nothing but a husband, but in
this 'nothing but' lies his right relationship with the divine order.
Indeed, his socialized identity may become the subjective 'locale'
of the sacred, or at least one such 'locale'. The awesomeness of
the sacred, posited as a reality 'behind' the phenomena of the
external world, is introjected into consciousness, mystifying the
formations of socialization that have been deposited there. Put
crudely, the individual is now in a position to shudder at himself.

The essence of all alienation is the imposition of a fictitious inexorability upon the humanly constructed world. The most important practical consequence of this is that empirical history and biography are falsely apprehended as grounded in supra-empirical necessities. The innumerable contingencies of human existence are transformed into inevitable manifestations of universal law. Activity becomes process. Choices become destiny. Men then live in the world they themselves have made as if they were fated to do so by powers that are quite independent of their own world-constructing enterprises. When alienation is religiously legitimated, the independence of these powers is vastly augmented, both in the collective nomos and in individual consciousness. The projected meanings of human activity congeal into a gigantic and mysterious 'other world', hovering over the world of men as an alien reality. By means of the 'otherness' of the sacred the alienation of the humanly constructed world is ultimately ratified. In as much as this inversion of the relationship between men and their world entails a denial of human choice, the encounter with the sacred is apprehended in terms of 'total dependence'.[25] This may or may not involve a masochistic attitude, though, as we have seen, the latter is an important motif of religious consciousness.

Now, it is important to recall here that the relationship between human activity and the world produced by it is and remains dialectical, *even when this fact is denied* (that is, when it is not present to consciousness). Thus men produce their gods even while they apprehend themselves as 'totally dependent' upon these their products. But, by the same token, the 'other world' of the gods takes on a certain autonomy *vis-à-vis* the human activity that ongoingly produces it. The supra-empirical reality posited by the religious projection is capable of acting back upon the empirical existence of men in society. Thus it would be gravely misleading to regard the religious formations as being simply mechanical effects of the activity that produced them, that is, as inert 'reflections' of their societal base.[26] On the contrary, the religious formations have the capacity to act upon and modify that base. This fact, however, has a curious consequence – namely, the possibility of *de-alienation itself being re-*

ligiously legitimated. Unless this possibility is grasped, a one-sided view of the relationship between religion and society is inevitable.[27] In other words, while religion has an intrinsic (and theoretically very understandable) tendency to legitimate alienation, there is also the possibility that de-alienation may be religiously legitimated in specific historical cases. The fact that, relative to the over-all tendency, the latter cases are somewhat rare does not detract from their theoretical interest.

Religion views institutions *sub specie aeternitatis.* We have seen how this tends to bestow a quality of immortality on these precarious formations of human history. It may also happen, though, that the same formations are radically *relativized,* precisely because they are viewed *sub specie aeternitatis.* This may take quite different forms in various religious traditions. For example, in some of the more sophisticated soteriologies of India the empirical world, including the social order and all its norms, appears as essentially an illusion, the realm of *maya,* nothing but an epiphenomenon *vis-à-vis* the ultimate reality of the *brahman-atman.* Inevitably, such a perspective relativizes the taken-for-granted institutional 'programmes' and, indeed, invalidates their traditional religious legitimations. The following passage from the Shvetashvatara Upanishad may serve as an illustration:

> Sacred poetry [*chandas*] – the sacrifices, the ceremonies, the ordinances,
> The past, the future, and what the Vedas declare –
> This whole world the illusion-maker [*mayin*] projects out of this [*Brahman*].
> And in it by illusion [*maya*] the other is confined.
> Now, one should know that Nature [*Prakriti*] is illusion [*maya*],
> And that the Mighty Lord [*mahesvara*] is the illusion-maker [*mayin*].[28]

To be sure, quite different practical implications may be drawn from this religiously induced scepticism about the common-sense verities. In the Indian soteriologies two typical implications have been the options of withdrawing from this illusion-world in the ascetic quest for liberation (*moksha*) and of continuing to act within it *as if* the traditional 'ceremonies and ordinances' still held, but doing so in an attitude of inner detachment from one's mundane activity – the classic distinction between the so-called 'way of knowledge' *jnana-marga* and 'way of action' *karma-marga*, the latter finding its most famous expression in the Bhagavad Gita.[29] Whatever the practical implications, the relativization inherent in the category of *maya* makes the socio-cultural world appear once more as a contingent, historical construction of men – a humanizing and thus at least potentially de-alienating effect.[30]

Mystical religion, with its radical depreciation not only of the value but the reality-status of the empirical world, has a similar de-alienating potential. To the mystic this world and all its works, including those of 'ordinary' religious practice, are relativized. In extreme cases this relativization may lead to a religiously legitimated anarchism, as in the antinomian movements of Christianity and Judaism. More commonly it leads to an 'as if' compliance with the 'ceremonies and ordinances' established in society, be it as a matter of convenience or out of consideration for the weaker spirit of the masses that has a need of these. The following passage from the *Theologia germanica* illustrates the latter attitude:

> Thus order, laws, precepts, and the like are merely an admonition to men who understand nothing better and know and perceive nothing else; therefore are all law and order ordained. And perfect men accept the law along with such ignorant men as understand and know nothing other or better, and practice it with them, to the intent that thereby they may be kept from evil ways, or if it be possible, brought to something higher.[31]

Again, different practical mandates may be drawn from such a perspective. It is not difficult to see that an antinomian mandate is likely to have potentially revolutionary consequences, while the outlook expressed in the above passage is rather likely to have a conservative effect. While these different possibilities are of great interest for a general sociology of religion, we cannot pursue them further here. The point here is, once more, that religious perspectives may *withdraw* the status of sanctity from institutions that were previously assigned this status by means of religious legitimation.

In the Biblical tradition the confrontation of the social order with the majesty of the transcendent God may also relativize this order to such an extent that one may validly speak of de-alienation – in the sense that, before the face of God, the institutions are revealed as nothing but *human* works, devoid of inherent sanctity or immorality. It was precisely this relativization of the social order and the concomitant disruption of the divine-human continuum that sharply set off Israel from the surrounding cultures of the ancient Near East.[32] An excellent example of this is the Israelite institution of kingship, which, compared with the institutions of sacred kingship in the surrounding cultures, constituted a kind of profanation.[33] The episode of the condemnation of David by Nathan (2 Samuel 12, 1–7) nicely shows the humanizing (and, *ipso facto,* de-alienating) consequence of this profanation – David is denied his royal prerogative of bad faith and addressed as just another man, responsible *as a man* for his actions.[34] Such a 'debunking' motif may be traced all through the Biblical tradition, directly related to its radical transcendentalization of God, finding its classic expression in Israelite prophecy but continuing in a variety of expressions in the history of the three great religions of the Biblical orbit. This same motif accounts for the recurrent revolutionary use of the Biblical tradition, against its (of course also recurrently attempted) employment for conservative legitimation. Just as there have been recurrent instances of kings mystifying their actions with the use of Biblical symbols, there have also been, over again, the Nathans who have unmasked them as very human mystifiers in the name of the same tradition from which the legitimating symbols derived.[35]

Just as institutions may be relativized and thus humanized when viewed *sub specie aeternitatis*, so may the roles representing these institutions. False consciousness and bad faith, widely legitimated by means of religion, may thus also be revealed as such by means of religion. Finally, and paradoxically, the entire web of religious mystifications thrown over the social order may, in certain cases, be drastically removed from the latter – *by religious means* – leaving it to be apprehended again as nothing but a human artifice. Both the radical depreciation of the empirical world in various traditions of mysticism and the radical transcendentalization of God in Biblical religion have been capable of leading to this result. As we shall try to indicate presently, the latter development has actually been historically instrumental in bringing about that global secularization of consciousness in which all the de-alienating perspectives of modern Western thought (including, incidentally, that of the sociological perspective) have their roots.

One may say, therefore, that religion appears in history both as a world-maintaining and as a world-shaking force. In both these appearances it has been both alienating and de-alienating – more commonly the first, because of intrinsic qualities of the religious enterprise as such, but in important instances the second. In all its manifestations, religion constitutes an immense projection of human meanings into the empty vastness of the universe – a projection, to be sure, which comes back as an alien reality to haunt its producers. Needless to say, it is impossible within the frame of reference of scientific theorizing to make any affirmations, positive *or* negative, about the ultimate ontological status of this alleged reality. Within this frame of reference, the religious projections can be dealt with only as such, as products of human activity and human consciousness, and rigorous brackets have to be placed around the question as to whether these projections may not *also* be something else than that (or, more accurately, *refer to* something else than the human world in which they empirically originate). In other words, every inquiry into religious matters that limits itself to the empirically available must necessarily be based on a '*methodological* atheism'.[36] But even within this inevitable methodological restraint one further point should be made once more: The religious enterprise of human history profoundly reveals the pressing urgency and intensity of man's quest for meaning. The gigantic projections of religious consciousness, whatever else they may be, constitute the historically most important effort of man to make reality humanly meaningful, at any price. Our discussion of religious masochism has indicated one price that has been paid for this. The great paradox of religious alienation is that the very process of dehumanizing the socio-cultural world has its roots in the fundamental wish that reality as a whole might have a meaningful place for man. One may thus say that alienation, too, has been a price paid by the religious consciousness in its quest for a humanly meaningful universe.

PART II

Historical Elements

5

The Process of
Secularization

Up to this point these considerations have been an exercise in
very broad theorizing. Historical material has been introduced to
illustrate general theoretical points, and not specifically to 'apply'
let alone 'validate' the latter. It is, of course, a moot question in
the social sciences to what extent theories of this degree of gen-
erality can be 'validated' at all and, therefore, whether they have
a place at all within the universe of discourse of the empirical
disciplines. This is not an appropriate occasion to enter this
methodological argument, and for the present purpose it matters
little whether the foregoing is considered as a preamble to the
sociologist's *opus proprium* or is itself dignified with the title of
sociological theory. It is clear, of course, that we would favour
the more expansive view that would permit our considerations to
be considered as sociological theory rather than as prolegomena
thereto. In any case, whatever one's conception of the scope of
sociologizing proper, it will be useful to see whether these theoretical perspectives can be of assistance in clarifying any given
empirical-historical situation, in other words, to see whether they
can be 'applied'. In this and the following chapters, then, the
attempt will be made to look at the contemporary religious situation from a vantage point given by our theoretical perspective.
Needless to say, no claim is implied that everything said here
about this situation derives from our own theoretical standpoint.
A variety of theoretical and empirical sources underlie our presentation. We would contend, however, that the foregoing theoretical perspective shows its utility by placing different aspects of
the situation in a new light and possibly by opening up some
previously neglected aspects to sociological scrutiny.

The term 'secularization' has had a somewhat adventurous history.[1] It was originally employed in the wake of the Wars of Religion to denote the removal of territory or property from the control of ecclesiastical authorities. In Roman canon law the same term has come to denote the return to the 'world' of a person in orders. In both these usages, whatever the disputes in particular instances, the term could be used in a purely descriptive and non-evaluative way. This, of course, has not been the case in the usage of more recent times. The term 'secularization', and even more its derivative 'secularism', has been employed as an ideological concept highly charged with evaluative connotations, sometimes positive and sometimes negative.[2] In anticlerical and 'progressive' circles it has come to stand for the liberation of modern man from religious tutelage, while in circles connected with the traditional churches it has been attacked as 'de-Christianization', 'paganization', and the like. Both these ideologically charged perspectives, within which the same empirical phenomena appear with opposite value indices, can be rather entertainingly observed in the work of sociologists of religion inspired, respectively, by Marxist and Christian viewpoints.[3] The situation has not been clarified by the fact that since the Second World War a number of theologians, mainly Protestants taking up certain strands in the later thought of Dietrich Bonhoeffer, have reversed the previous Christian evaluation of 'secularization' and hailed it as a realization of crucial motifs of Christianity itself.[4] Not surprisingly the position has been advanced that, in view of this ideological furore, the term should be abandoned as confusing if not downright meaningless.[5]

We would not agree with this position, despite the justification of the ideological analysis on which it is based. The term 'secularization' refers to empirically available processes of great importance in modern Western history. Whether these processes are to be deplored or welcomed is, of course, irrelevant within the universe of discourse of the historian or the sociologist. It is possible, actually without too great an effort, to describe the empirical phenomenon without taking up an evaluative stance. It is also possible to inquire into its historical origins, *including* its historical connection with Christianity, without asserting that this represents either a fulfilment or a degeneration of the latter. This point should be particularly stressed in view of the current discussion among theologians. It is one thing to maintain that there is a relationship of historical causality between Christianity and certain features of the modern world. It is an altogether different matter to say that, 'therefore', the modern world, including its secular character, must be seen as some sort of logical realization of Christianity. A salutary thing to remember in this connection is that most historical relationships are ironical in character, or, to put it differently, that the course of history has little to do with the intrinsic logic of ideas that served as causal factors in it.[6]

It is not difficult to put forth a simple definition of secularization for the purpose at hand. By secularization we mean the process by which sectors of society and culture are removed from the domination of religious institutions and symbols. When we speak of society and institutions in modern Western history, of course, secularization manifests itself in the evacuation by the Christian Churches of areas previously under their control or influence – as in the separation of Church and state, or in the expropriation of Church lands, or in the emancipation of education from ecclesiastical authority. When we speak of culture and symbols, however, we imply that secularization is more than a social-structural process. It affects the totality of cultural life and of ideation, and may be observed in the decline of religious contents in the arts, in philosophy, in literature and, most important of all, in the rise of science as an autonomous, thoroughly secular perspective on the world. Moreover, it is implied here that the process of secularization has a subjective side as well. As there is a secularization of society and culture, so is there a secularization of consciousness. Put simply, this means that the modern West has produced an increasing number of individuals who look upon the world and their own lives without the benefit of religious interpretations.

While secularization may be viewed as a global phenomenon of modern societies, it is not uniformly distributed within them.

Different groups of the population have been affected by it differently.[7] Thus it has been found that the impact of secularization has tended to be stronger on men than on women, on people in the middle age range than on the very young and the old, in the cities than in the country, on classes directly connected with modern industrial production (particularly the working class) than on those of more traditional occupations (such as artisans or small shopkeepers), on Protestants and Jews than on Catholics, and the like. At least as far as Europe is concerned, it is possible to say with some confidence, on the basis of these data, that Church-related religiosity is strongest (and thus, at any rate, social-structural secularization least) on the margins of modern industrial society, both in terms of marginal classes (such as the remnants of old petty bourgeoisies) and marginal individuals (such as those eliminated from the work process).[8] The situation is different in America, where the Churches still occupy a more central symbolic position, but it may be argued that they have succeeded in keeping this position only by becoming highly secularized themselves, so that the European and American cases represent two variations on the same underlying theme of global secularization.[9] What is more, it appears that the same secularizing forces have now become world-wide in the course of Westernization and modernization.[10] Most of the available data, to be sure, pertain to structural manifestations of secularization rather than to the secularization of consciousness, but we have enough data to indicate the massive presence of the latter in the contemporary West.[11] We cannot here pursue the interesting question of the extent to which there may be, so to speak, asymmetry between these two dimensions of secularization, so that there may not only be secularization of consciousness within the traditional religious institutions but also a continuation of more or less traditional motifs of religious consciousness outside their previous institutional contexts.[12]

If, for heuristic purposes, we were to take an epidemiological viewpoint with regard to secularization, it would be natural to ask what are its 'carriers'.[13] In other words, what socio-cultural processes and groups serve as vehicles or mediators of secularization? Viewed from outside Western civilization (say, by a concerned Hindu traditionalist), the answer is obviously that it is that civilization as a whole in its spread around the world (and it need hardly be emphasized that, from that viewpoint, Communism and modern nationalism are just as much manifestations of Westernization as their 'imperialist' predecessors). Viewed from inside Western civilization (say, by a worried Spanish country priest), the original 'carrier' of secularization is the modern economic process, that is, the dynamic of industrial capitalism. To be sure, it may be 'secondary' effects of this dynamic that constitute the immediate problem (for example, the secularizing contents of modern mass media or the influences of a heterogeneous mass of tourists brought in by modern means of transportation). But it does not take long to trace these 'secondary' effects back to their original source in the expanding capitalist-industrial economy. In those parts of the Western world where industrialism has taken socialist forms of organization, closeness to the processes of industrial production and its concomitant styles of life continues to be the principal determinant of secularization.[14] Today, it would seem, it is industrial society in itself that is secularizing, with its divergent ideological legitimations serving merely as modifications of the global secularization process. Thus the anti-religious propaganda and repressive measures of Marxist regimes naturally affect the secularization process (though, perhaps, not always in quite the way intended by their initiators), as do the pro-religious policies of various governments outside the Marxist sphere. It seems likely, however, that both these political-ideological attitudes must reckon with basic societal forces that antedate the particular policies in question and over which governments have only limited control. This state of affairs becomes amusingly evident when we see very similar sociological data for socialist and non-socialist countries (say, with regard to the secularity of the working class and the religiosity of the peasants) used by Marxist observers as an occasion to bemoan the limited effectiveness of 'scientific atheist' agitation and by Christian observers to lament the failures of evangelism, to the point where one is tempted to suggest that the two groups might get together and comfort each other.

We would regard it as axiomatic that a historical phenomenon of such scope will not be amenable to any monocausal explanations. Thus we have no interest in denigrating any of the various factors that have been suggested as causes of secularization (such as, for example, the pervasive influence of modern science). Nor are we interested, in the present context, in the establishment of a hierarchy of causes. We are interested, however, in the question of the extent to which the Western religious tradition may have carried the seeds of secularization within itself. If this can be maintained, as we think it can, it should be clear from our systematic considerations that the religious factor must *not* be considered as operating in isolation from other factors, but rather as standing in an ongoing dialectical relationship with the 'practical' infrastructure of social life. In other words, nothing could be farther from our minds than to propose an 'idealist' explanation of secularizing. It should also be clear that any demonstration of the secularizing consequences of the Western religious tradition tells us nothing about the intentions of those who shaped and carried on this tradition.[15]

The suspicion that there may be an inherent connection between Christianity and the character of the modern Western world is by no means new. At least since Hegel the connection has been repeatedly asserted by historians, philosophers, theologians, though, of course, their evaluation of this has varied greatly. Thus the modern world could be interpreted as a higher realization of the Christian spirit (as Hegel interpreted it), or Christianity could be regarded as the principal pathogenic factor responsible for the supposedly sorry state of the modern world (as, for instance, by Schopenhauer and Nietzsche). The notion that a peculiar role in the establishment of the modern world was played by Protestantism has, of course, been a matter of widespread discussion among sociologists and historians for the last fifty years or so. It may be useful, though, to briefly summarize this notion here.[16]

If compared with the 'fulness' of the Catholic universe, Protestantism appears as radical truncation, a reduction to 'essentials' at the expense of a vast wealth of religious contents. This is especially true of the Calvinist version of Protestantism, but to a considerable degree the same may be said of the Lutheran and even the Anglican Reformation. Our statement, of course, is merely descriptive – we are not interested in whatever theological justifications there may be either for the Catholic *pleroma* or for the evangelical sparseness of Protestantism. If we look at these two religious constellations more carefully, though, Protestant-ism may be described in terms of an immense shrinkage in the scope of the sacred in reality, as compared with its Catholic adversary. The sacramental apparatus is reduced to a minimum and, even there, divested of its more numinous qualities. The miracle of the mass disappears altogether. Less routine miracles, if not denied altogether, lose all real significance for the religious life. The immense network of intercession that unites the Cath-olic in this world with the saints and, indeed, with all departed souls disappears as well. Protestantism ceased praying for the dead. At the risk of some simplification, it can be said that Prot-estantism divested itself as much as possible from the three most ancient and most powerful concomitants of the sacred – mystery, miracle, and magic. This process has been aptly caught in the phrase 'disenchantment of the world'.[17] The Protestant believer no longer lives in a world ongoingly penetrated by sacred beings and forces. Reality is polarized between a radically transcendent divinity and a radically 'fallen' humanity that, *ipso facto*, is devoid of sacred qualities. Between them lies an altogether 'natu-ral' universe, God's creation to be sure, but in itself bereft of numinosity. In other words, the radical transcendence of God confronts a universe of radical immanence, of 'closedness' to the sacred. Religiously speaking, the world becomes very lonely indeed.

The Catholic lives in a world in which the sacred is mediated to him through a variety of channels – the sacraments of the Church, the intercession of the saints, the recurring eruption of the 'supernatural' in miracles – a vast continuity of being be-tween the seen and the unseen. Protestantism abolished most of these mediations. It broke the continuity, cut the umbilical cord between heaven and earth, and thereby threw man back upon himself in a historically unprecedented manner. Needless to say, this was not its intention. It only denuded the world of divinity in order to emphasize the terrible majesty of the transcendent God and it only threw man into total 'fallenness' in order to make him open to the intervention of God's sovereign grace, the only true miracle in the Protestant universe. In doing this, however, it narrowed man's relationship to the sacred to the one exceedingly narrow channel that it called God's word (not to be identified with a fundamentalist conception of the Bible, but rather with the uniquely redemptive action of God's grace – the *sola gratia* of the Lutheran confessions). As long as the plausibility of this conception was maintained, of course, secularization was effectively arrested, even though all its ingredients were already present in the Protestant universe. It needed only the cutting of this one narrow channel of mediation, though, to open the floodgates of secularization. In other words, with nothing remaining 'in between' a radically transcendent God and a radically immanent human world *except* this one channel, the sinking of the latter into implausibility left an empirical reality in which, indeed, 'God is dead'. This reality then became amenable to the systematic, rational penetration, both in thought and in activity, which we associate with modern science and technology. A sky empty of angels becomes open to the intervention of the astronomer and, eventually, of the astronaut. It may be maintained, then, that Protestantism served as a historically decisive prelude to secularization, whatever may have been the importance of other factors.

If this interpretation of the historical nexus between Protestantism and secularization is accepted (as it probably is today by a majority of scholarly opinion), then the question inevitably suggests itself as to whether the secularizing potency of Protestantism was a *novum* or whether it rather had its roots in earlier elements of the Biblical tradition. We would contend that the latter answer is the correct one, indeed that the roots of secularization are to be found in the earliest available sources for the religion of ancient Israel. In other words, we would maintain that the 'disenchantment of the world' begins in the Old Testament.[18]

In order to appreciate this position one must see ancient Israel in the context of the cultures amid which it sprang up and *against* which it defined itself.[19] While it would be erroneous to underestimate the considerable differences between these cultures (notably between the two cultural foci of Egypt and Mesopotamia), one common characteristic is the one that has aptly been called 'cosmological'.[20] This means that the human world (that is, everything that we today would call culture and society) is understood as being embedded in a cosmic order that embraces the entire universe. This order not only fails to make the sharp modern differentiation between the human and non-human (or 'natural') spheres of empirical reality, but, more importantly, it is an order that posits continuity between the empirical and the supra-empirical, between the world of men and the world of the gods. This continuity, which assumes an ongoing linkage of human events with the sacred forces permeating the universe, is realized (not just reaffirmed but literally re-established) again and again in religious ritual. For example, in the great New Year festival of ancient Mesopotamia the creation of the world is not only represented (as we today might understand it in terms of some sort of symbolism) but once more realized, made a reality, as human life is brought back again to its divine source. Thus everything that happens 'here below' on the human plane has its analogue 'up above' on the plane of the gods, and everything that happens 'now' is linked with the cosmic events that occurred 'in the beginning'.[21] This continuity between the human microcosm and the divine macrocosm can, of course, be broken, particularly by misdeeds on the part of men. Such misdeeds may be of the sort we today would call 'unethical' or 'sinful', but they might also be of a quite different kind, such as in the breaking of taboos or in the improper performance of sacred ceremonies. In such cases the cosmic order has been 'wronged' – and must again be 'righted' by the appropriate ritual and moral acts. For example, disobedience to the god-king of Egypt is not only a political or ethical malfeasance, but a disturbance of the cosmic order of things (expressed as *ma'at* by the Egyptians) that may affect the annual flooding of the Nile as much as the proper functioning of social relations or the safety of the frontiers – its 'correction', then, is not only a matter of just punishment of the malfeasant but of the re-establishment of the proper relationship between the land of Egypt and the cosmic order on which it rests. To use two terms discussed previously, human affairs are on-goingly nomized by means of cosmization, that is, by being brought back into the cosmic order outside of which there is nothing but chaos.[22]

One point that should be strongly emphasized is that this sort of universe is one of great security for the individual. Put negatively, it is a universe furnishing highly effective barriers against anomy. This does not mean at all that nothing terrible could happen to the individual or that he is guaranteed perennial happiness. It does mean that whatever happens, however terrible, *makes sense* to him by being related to the ultimate meaning of things. Only if this point is grasped can one understand the persistent attractiveness of the various versions of this world view to the Israelites, even long after their own religious development had decisively broken with it. Thus, for instance, it would be very misleading to think that the persistent attraction of sacred prostitution (against which the spokesmen of Yahweh thundered for centuries) was a matter of mundane lust. After all, we may assume that there were plenty of *non*-sacred prostitutes around (to which, it seems, Yahweh's objections were minimal). The attraction rather lay in an altogether religious desire, namely in the nostalgia for the continuity between man and the cosmos that was sacramentally mediated by sacred sexuality.

It is profoundly significant that the traditions later incorporated in the canon of the Old Testament interpreted the origins of Israel as a *double* exodus – the patriarchs' exodus from Mesopotamia and the great exodus from Egypt under Moses. This prototypical Israelite exodus was not just a geographical or political movement. Rather, it constituted a break with an entire universe. At the heart of the religion of ancient Israel lies the

vehement repudiation of both the Egyptian and the Mesopotamian versions of cosmic order, a repudiation that was, of
course, extended to the pre-Israelite indigenous culture of Syria-
Palestine. The 'fleshpots of Egypt', from which Yahweh led
Israel into the desert, stood above all for the security of the
cosmic order in which Egyptian culture was rooted. Israel
defined itself as separation from that cosmic unity that the Mem-
phite Theology (in many ways the *magna charta* of Egyptian civilization) identified with the divinity Ptah – 'for everything came
forth from him, nourishment and provisions, the offerings of the
gods, and every good thing'.[23] This great denial of Israelite religion may be analysed in terms of three pervasive motifs – transcendentalization, historization, and the rationalization of
ethics.[24]

The Old Testament posits a God who stands *outside* the
cosmos, which is his creation but which he confronts and does
not permeate. It is not very easy to decide at what point in the
religious development of ancient Israel there emerged that conception of God which we now associate with Judeo-Christian
monotheism. By the eighth century, at the very latest, we find
that conception fully developed and radically divergent from the
general religious conceptions of the ancient Near East. This God
is radically transcendent, not to be identified with any natural or
human phenomena. He is not only the creator of the world but
the *only* God – if not the only one in existence, at any rate the
only one who mattered for Israel. He appears without mates or
offspring, unaccompanied by a pantheon of any sort. Furthermore, this God acts historically rather than cosmically, particularly though not exclusively in the history of Israel, and he is
a God of radical ethical demands. But even if we cannot completely identify the earlier Israelite conceptions of its God with
the one we find expressed by Amos, Hosea, and Isaiah in the
eighth century, there are certain features that it apparently pos-
sessed from the earliest times, probably antedating the coming of
the Israelite tribes to Palestine. Yahweh, whatever he may have
been before his 'adoption' by Israel (a process that, of course,
Israel viewed as *its* adoption by *him*), was for Israel a God from far

away. He was not a local or tribal divinity 'naturally' connected with Israel, but a God linked to Israel 'artificially', that is, historically. This linkage was established by the covenant between Yahweh and Israel, a relationship that entailed very specific obligations for Israel and one that could be abrogated if these obligations were not fulfilled (*that*, indeed, was the terrible message of eighth-century prophecy). Yahweh was consequently a 'mobile' God, who could not be tied down either geographically or institutionally – he had *chosen* Palestine as the land of Israel, but he was not tied to it – he had *chosen* Saul and David as kings over Israel, but the monarchy was by no means an institution of divinity in the Egyptian or even the (modified) Mesopotamian sense. This 'mobility' of Yahweh was well expressed in the portable character of the ark of the covenant, which was only 'accidentally' deposited in this or that sanctuary, but even when it finally came to rest in the temple at Jerusalem the latter could in no way be regarded as Yahweh's necessary habitat (with the tremendously important consequence that Israel survived the destruction of Jerusalem first by the Babylonians and then, in a different form, by the Romans). This God demanded sacrifice, but he was not dependent upon it. And, consequently, he was fundamentally immune to magical manipulation.[25]

The radical transcendentalization of God in the Old Testament can be best seen in precisely those places where elements of extra-Israelite religion are incorporated. A good example is the creation story of Genesis 1, which incorporates a number of cosmogonic elements from Mesopotamian mythology. However interesting these may be for the historian of religion, even a cursory comparison with the Enuma Elish, the great Akkadian creation epic, brings out sharply the transformation of these elements at the hand of the Israelite adaptors. There we find a luxuriant world of gods and their deeds – here the lonely action of the creating God. There the divine forces of creation spring themselves from primeval chaos – here there is nothing before God, whose act of creation is the beginning of all things, with chaos (the *tohu vavohu* of the Genesis text) reduced to mere negativity awaiting the actions of God. Even in the one place of the Genesis account in which there remains the unmistakable trace of a mythological name – the *tehom*, the 'deep' over which there was darkness, a Hebrew cognate of the name of the Mesopotamian goddess Tiamat from whose waters the gods were formed – this has been reduced to an abstract metaphysical category. And, significantly, the Genesis account ends with the creation of man as a being highly distinct from all other creatures, that is, in emphatic *dis*continuity not only with God but with the rest of creation. We find here expressed very clearly the fundamental Biblical polarization between the transcendent God and man, with a thoroughly 'demythologized' universe between them.[26]

The historization motif is already implied in this polarization. The world, bereft of mythologically conceived divine forces, becomes the arena on the one hand of God's great acts (that is, the arena of *Heilsgeschichte*) and on the other of the activity of highly individuated men (that is, the arena of 'profane history'), who populate the pages of the Old Testament to a degree unique in ancient religious literature. Israel's faith was a *historic* one from the earliest sources to their canonical codification.[27] It referred above all to a series of historically specific events – the exodus from Egypt, the establishment of the covenant at Sinai, the taking of the land. Thus the first known 'creed' of ancient Israel, the text now contained in Deuteronomy 26, 5–9, is nothing but a recital of historical events, all, of course, attributed to acts of God. It may be said, without too gross exaggeration, that the entire Old Testament – 'Torah, prophets, and "writings" ' – is but an immense elaboration of this creed. There are almost no books now contained in the Old Testament that are devoid of historical orientation, either directly or by rootage in the historically oriented cult (the two clear exceptions, Ecclesiastes and Job, are characteristically very late). About one half of the Old Testament corpus is occupied by the 'historiographic' works proper – Hexateuch, Kings, and Chronicles, with other purely historical works such as Esther. The orientation of the prophetic books is overwhelmingly historical. The Psalms are rooted in a cult constantly referring to the historic acts of God, as most clearly expressed in the annual cycle of Israelite festivals. The Old Testament revolves around history in a way no other great book of world religion does (*not*, incidentally, excluding the New Testament).

It may be said that the transcendentalization of God and the concomitant 'disenchantment of the world' opened up a 'space' for history as the arena of both divine and human actions. The former are performed by a God standing entirely outside the world. The latter presuppose a considerable individualism in the conception of man. Man appears as this historical actor before the face of God (something quite different, by the way, from man as the actor in the face of fate, as in Greek tragedy). Thus individual men are seen less and less as representatives of mythologically conceived collectivities, as was typical of archaic thought, but as distinct and unique individuals, performing important acts *as* individuals. One may only think here of such highly profiled figures as Moses, David, Elijah, and so forth. This is true even of such figures as may be the result of 'demythologizations' of originally semi-divine figures, such as the patriarchs or heroes like Samson (possibly derived from the Canaanite god Shamash). This is *not* to suggest that the Old Testament meant what the modern West means by 'individualism', nor even the conception of the individual attained in Greek philosophy, but that it provided a religious framework for a conception of the individual, his dignity and his freedom of action. There is no need to stress the world-historical importance of this, but it is important to see it in connection with the roots of secularization that interest us here.

The development of a grand theology of history in the prophetic literature of the Old Testament is too well known to require elaboration here. But it is well to see that the same historicity pertains to cult and law in ancient Israel. The two major cultic festivals of the Old Testament constitute historizations of previously mythologically legitimated occasions. The Passover, originally (that is, in its extra-Israelite origins) the feast celebrating divine fertility, becomes the celebration of the exodus. The New Year festival (including Yom Kippur), originally the re-enactment of cosmogonic myths, becomes the celebration of Yahweh's kingship over Israel. The same historicity pertains to the lesser festivals. Old Testament law and ethics are also located in a historical framework, in that they always relate to obligations arising for Israel and the individual Israelite from the covenant with Yahweh. In other words, by contrast with the rest of the ancient Near East, law and ethics are *not* grounded in a timeless cosmic order (as in the Egyptian *ma'at*), but in the concrete and historically mediated commandments of the 'living God'. It is in this sense that one must understand the recurrent phrase of condemnation, 'Such a thing is not done in Israel'. Similar phrases of course, may be found in other cultures, but here they refer precisely to that law that was, historically, 'given to Moses'. It is on the basis of these very early presuppositions that the Israelite view of history developed, from the original faith in the election of the people by Yahweh to the monumental theodicies of history and eschatologies of the later prophets.

The motif of ethical rationalization in the Old Testament (in the sense of imposing rationality on life) is closely related to the two other motifs just described.[28] A rationalizing element was present from the beginning, above all because of the anti-magical animus of Yahwism. This element was 'carried' by both priestly and prophetic groups. The priestly ethic (as in its monumental expression in Deuteronomy) was rationalizing in its purge from the cult of all magical and orgiastic elements, as well as in its development of religious law (*torah*) as the fundamental discipline of everyday life. The prophetic ethic was rationalizing in its insistence on the totality of life as service to God, thus imposing a cohesive and, *ipso facto*, rational structure upon the whole spectrum of everyday activities. The same prophetic ethic provided the peculiar theodicy of history (as especially in Deutero-Isaiah) that allowed Israel to survive the catastrophe of the Babylonian exile, after which, however, one may say that its historical efficacy was 'exhausted'. The priestly ethic (which, to be sure, was strongly influenced by the prophetic teachings) went on to develop the cultic and legal institutions around which the post-exilic community could be reconstituted under Ezra and Nehemiah. The legal institutions, constituting the peculiar structure of what then became Judaism, finally proved capable of surviving even the end of the cult, following the destruction of the second temple by the Romans. Diaspora Judaism may be regarded as a triumph of rationality, in a specifically juridical sense. Because of its marginal character within the context of Western culture, however, it would be difficult to maintain that diaspora Judaism played an important role in the rationalization processes at the roots of the modern world. It is more plausible to assume that the rationalizing motif achieved efficacy in the formation of the modern West by means of its transmission by Christianity.

Needless to say, it has not been our purpose in the preceding pages to give a thumbnail sketch of Israelite religious history. We have simply tried to give some indications that the 'disenchantment of the world', which has created unique nomic problems for the modern West, has roots that greatly antedate the events of the Reformation and the Renaissance that are commonly regarded as its starting points. Equally needless to say, we cannot try here to give an account of the manner in which the secularizing potency of Biblical religion, combined with other factors, came to fruition in the modern West. Only a few comments can be made about this.[29]

Whatever may have been the religious character of Jesus and his earliest followers, there seems little question but that the form of Christianity that finally became dominant in Europe represents a retrogressive step in terms of the secularizing motifs of Old Testament religion (a descriptive statement to which, of course, no evaluative intent on our part should be attached). While the transcendent character of God is strongly asserted, the very notion of the incarnation and then even more its theoretical development in trinitarian doctrine represent significant modifications in the radicality of the Israelite conception. This point was seen more clearly by the Jewish and Muslim critics of Christianity than by those standing within the Christian camp. Thus there is some justification (again, of course, in a purely descriptive sense) in the classic Muslim view that the essence of the Christian 'apostasy' from true monotheism is in the doctrine of *hullul* – 'incarnationism', as the idea that anything or anyone could stand beside God, or serve as a mediator between God and Man. Perhaps it is not surprising that the central Christian notion of incarnation brought in its wake a multiplicity of other modifications of transcendence, the whole host of angels and saints with which Catholicism populated religious reality, culminating in the glorification of Mary as mediator and co-redeemer. In the measure that the divine transcendence was modified, the world was 're-enchanted' (or, if one wishes, 're-mythologized'). We would contend, indeed, that Catholicism succeeded in re-establishing a new version of cosmic order in a gigantic synthesis of Biblical religion with extra-Biblical cosmological conceptions. In this view, the crucial Catholic doctrine of the *analogia entis* between God and man, between heaven and earth, constitutes a replication of the mimesis of archaic, pre-Biblical religion. Whatever their other important differences may be, we would see both Latin and Greek Catholicism performing essentially the same replication on this level. It is precisely in this sense that the Catholic universe is a secure one for its 'inhabitants' – and for this reason of intense attractiveness to this day. It is in the same sense that Catholicism may be understood as the continuing presence in the modern world of some of the most ancient religious aspirations of man.

By the same token, Catholicism arrested the process of ethical rationalization. To be sure, Latin Catholicism absorbed a highly rational legalism inherited from Rome, but its pervasive sacramental system provided innumerable 'escape hatches' from the sort of total rationalization of life demanded by Old Testament prophecy or, indeed, by rabbinical Judaism. Ethical absolutism of the prophetic variety was more or less safely segregated in the institutions of monasticism, thus kept from 'contaminating' the body of Christendom as a whole. Again, the starkness of the Israelite religious conceptions was modified, mellowed, except for those chosen few who chose the ascetic life. On the theoretical level, the Catholic view of natural law may be said to represent a 're-naturalization' of ethics – in a sense, a return to the divine-human continuity of Egyptian *ma'at* from which Israel went out

into the desert of Yahweh. On the practical level, Catholic piety
and morality provided a way of life that made unnecessary any
radical rationalization of the world.[30]

But whereas it can be plausibly argued that Christianity,
specifically in its victorious Catholic form, reversed or at least
arrested the secularizing motifs of transcendentalization and
ethical rationalization, this cannot be said of the motif of historization. Latin Christianity in the West, at any rate, remained
thoroughly historical in its view of the world. It retained the
peculiarly Biblical theodicy of history and, except for those mystical movements that (as everywhere in the orbit of Biblically
derived monotheism) always moved on the periphery of heresy,
rejected those religious constructions that would despair of this
world as the arena of redemption. Catholic Christianity thus
carried within it the seeds of the revolutionary impetus, even if
this often remained dormant for long periods under the 'cos-
micizing' effects of the Catholic universe. It erupted again and
again in a variety of chiliastic movements, though its release as a
force of world-historical dimensions had to await the disintegration of Christendom as a viable plausibility structure for
Western man.

There is another central characteristic of Christianity that,
again in a most unintended manner, eventually served the
process of secularization – the social formation of the Christian
Church. In terms of the comparative sociology of religion, the
Christian Church represents a very unusual case of the institutional specialization of religion, that is, of an institution
specifically concerned with religion in counterposition with all
other institutions of society.[31] Such a development is relatively
rare in the history of religion, where the more common state of
affairs is a diffusion of religious activities and symbols throughout the institutional fabric, though the Christian case is not
unique (for example, in quite a different way, the Buddhist
sangha represents another case of such institutional specialization). The concentration of religious activities and symbols in
one institutional sphere, however, *ipso facto* defines the rest of
society as 'the world', as a profane realm at least relatively re-

moved from the jurisdiction of the sacred. The secularizing potential of this conception could be 'contained' as long as Christendom, with its sensitive balance of the sacred and the profane, existed as a social reality. With the disintegration of this reality, however, 'the world' could all the more rapidly be secularized in that it had already been defined as a realm outside the jurisdiction of the sacred properly speaking. The logical development of this may be seen in the Lutheran doctrine of the two kingdoms, in which the autonomy of the secular 'world' is actually given a *theological* legitimation.[32]

If we look at the great religious constellations derived from the Old Testament, therefore, we find quite differential relationships to the latter's secularizing forces. Judaism appears as an encapsulation of these forces in a highly rationalized but historically ineffective formation, the ineffectiveness to be ascribed both to the extrinsic factor of the fate of the Jews as an alien people within Christendom and the intrinsic factor of the conservative impact of Jewish legalism. In this latter respect Islam bears a close resemblance to Judaism, with the obvious difference that it succeeded in imposing its conservatory structures not just within a segregated subculture but over an empire of vast geographical expanse.[33] Catholic Christianity, both Latin and Greek, may be seen as an arresting and retrogressive step in the unfolding of the drama of secularization, although it preserved within it (at least in the Latin West) the secularizing potential, if only by virtue of its preservation of the Old Testament canon (decided upon once and for all in the rejection of the Marcionite heresy). The Protestant Reformation, however, may then be understood as a powerful re-emergence of precisely those secularizing forces that had been 'contained' by Catholicism, not only replicating the Old Testament in this, but going decisively beyond it. To what extent the historical coincidence of the impact of Protestantism with that of the Renaissance, with its resurgence of the quite different secularizing forces of classical antiquity, was simply an accident or rather a mutually dependent phenomenon cannot be pursued here. Nor can we try to weigh here the relative effect of Protestantism as against other factors, both 'ideal' and 'material', in the process of secularization of the last 400 years. All we wanted to indicate was that the question, 'Why in the modern West?' asked with respect to the phenomenon of secularization, must be answered at least in part by looking at its roots in the religious tradition of the modern West.

In terms of the general socio-religious processes discussed in the first part of this book, secularization has posited an altogether novel situation for modern man. Probably for the first time in history, the religious legitimations of the world have lost their plausibility not only for a few intellectuals and other marginal individuals, but for broad masses of entire societies. This opened up an acute crisis not only for the nomization of the large social institutions but for that of individual biographies. In other words, there has arisen a problem of 'meaningfulness' not only for such institutions as the state or the economy but for the ordinary routines of everyday life. The problem has, of course, been intensely conscious to various theoreticians (philosophers, theologians, psychologists, and so forth), but there is good reason to think that it is also prominent in the minds of ordinary people not normally given to theoretical speculations and interested simply in solving the crises of their own lives. Most importantly, the peculiar Christian theodicy of suffering lost its plausibility and thereby the way was opened for a variety of secularized soteriologies, most of which, however, proved quite incapable of legitimating the sorrows of individual life even when they achieved some plausibility in the legitimation of history. And finally the collapse of the alienated structures of the Christian world view released movements of critical thought that rad- ically de-alienated and 'humanized' social reality (the sociological perspective being one of these movements), an achievement that often enough was bought at the price of severe anomy and existen- tial anxiety. What all of this means for contemporary society is the principal question for an empirical sociology of knowledge. Within our present considerations we cannot deal with all this except tangentially. The question, though, that we will turn to next is what the process of secularization has meant for the tradi- tional religious contents and for the institutions that embody them.

6

Secularization and the Problem of Plausibility

One of the most obvious ways in which secularization has affected the man in the street is as a 'crisis of credibility' in religion. Put differently, secularization has resulted in a widespread collapse of the plausibility of traditional religious definitions of reality. This manifestation and secularization on the level of consciousness ('subjective secularization', if one wishes) has its correlate on the social-structural level (as 'objective secularization'). Subjectively, the man in the street tends to be uncertain about religious matters. Objectively, the man in the street is confronted with a wide variety of religious and other reality-defining agencies that compete for his allegiance or at least attention, and none of which is in a position to coerce him into allegiance. In other words, the phenomenon called 'pluralism' is a social-structural correlate of the secularization of consciousness. This relationship invites sociological analysis.[1]

Such analysis affords a very nice opportunity to show *in concreto* the dialectical relationship between religion and its infrastructure that has previously been developed theoretically. It is possible to analyse secularization in such a way that it appears as a 'reflection' of concrete infrastructural processes in modern society. This is all the more convincing because secularization appears to be a 'negative' phenomenon, that is, it seems to be without causal efficacy of its own and continually dependent upon processes other than itself. Such an analysis, however, remains convincing only if the contemporary situation is viewed in isolation from its historical background. Religion under the impact of secularization can, indeed, be analysed convincingly as a 'dependent variable' *today*. As soon, though, as one asks about the historical origins of secularization the problem poses itself in quite different terms. As we have tried to indicate, one is then led to consider specific elements of the religious tradition of Western culture precisely as historical forces, that is, as 'independent variables'.

The dialectical relationship between religion and society thus precludes the doctrinaire approaches of either 'idealism' or 'materialism'. It is possible to show in concrete instances how religious 'ideas', even very abstruse ones, led to empirically available changes in the social structure. In other instances, it is possible to show how empirically available structural changes had effects on the level of religious consciousness and ideation. Only a dialectical understanding of these relationships avoids the distortions of the one-sidedly 'idealist' and 'materialist' interpretations. Such a dialectical understanding will insist upon the rootage of all consciousness, religious or other, in the world of everyday *praxis,* but it will be very careful not to conceive of this rootage in terms of mechanistic causality.[2]

A quite different matter is the potency of religion to 'act back' upon its infrastructure in specific historical situations. On this it is possible to say that such potency varies greatly in different situations. Thus religion might appear as a formative force in one situation and as a dependent formation in the situation following historically.[3] One may describe such change as a 'reversal' in the 'direction' of causal efficacy as between religion and its respective infrastructures. The phenomenon under consideration here is a case in point. Religious developments originating in the Biblical tradition may be seen as causal factors in the formation of the modern secularized world. Once formed, however, this world precisely precludes the continuing efficacy of religion as a formative force. We would contend that here lies the great historical irony in the relation between religion and secularization, an irony that can be graphically put by saying that, historically speaking, Christianity has been its own gravedigger. In looking at the collapse of plausibility suffered by religion in the contemporary situation, *hic et nunc,* it is logical to begin with social structure and to go on to consciousness and ideation, rather than the reverse. Quite apart from its theoretical justification, this procedure will avoid the pitfall (to which religiously inclined observers are particularly prone) of ascribing secularization to some mysterious spiritual and intellectual fall from grace. Rather it will show the rootage of this fall from grace (the term is descriptively useful) in empirically available social-structural processes.

The original 'locale' of secularization, as we have indicated, was in the economic area, specifically, in those sectors of the economy being formed by the capitalistic and industrial processes. Consequently, different strata of modern society have been affected by secularization differentially in terms of their closeness to or distance from these processes. Highly secularized strata emerged in the immediate proximity of these same processes. In other words, modern industrial society has produced a centrally 'located' sector that is something like a 'liberated territory' with respect to religion. Secularization has moved 'outwards' from this sector into other areas of society. One interesting consequence of this has been a tendency for religion to be 'polarized' between the most public and the most private sectors of the institutional order, specifically between the institutions of the state and the family. Even at a point of far-reaching secularization of everyday life as lived at work and in the relationships that surround work one may still find religious symbols attached to the institutions of state and family. For instance, at a point where everyone takes for granted that 'religion stops at the factory gate', it may nevertheless be also taken for granted that one does not inaugurate either a war or a marriage without the traditional religious symbolizations.[4]

A way of putting this in terms of common sociological parlance is to say that there has been a 'cultural lag' between the secularization of the economy on the one hand and that of the state and the family on the other. As far as the state is concerned, this has meant the continuation in several countries of traditional religious legitimations of the political order at a time when those countries were already well on the way towards becoming modern industrial societies. This was certainly the case with

England, the first country to embark on this journey. On the other hand, secularizing political forces have been at work in countries that still lagged behind in terms of capitalistic-industrial development, as in France in the late eighteenth century and in many of the underdeveloped countries today. The relationship between socio-economic modernization and political secularization, therefore, is not a simple one. Nevertheless, we would contend that there is a tendency towards the secularization of the political order that goes naturally with the development of modern industrialism. Specifically, there is a tendency towards the institutional separation between the state and religion. Whether this is a practical matter originally unconnected with ideological anti-clericalism, as in America, or is linked to an anti-clerical or even anti-religious *'laïcisme'*, as in France, is dependent upon peculiar historical factors at work in different national societies. The global tendency seems to be in all cases the emergence of a state emancipated from the sway of either religious institutions or religious rationales of political action. This is also true in those 'antiquarian' cases in which the same political secularization continues to be decorated with the traditional symbols of religio-political unity, as in England or Sweden. Indeed, the anachronism of the traditional symbols in these cases only serves to underline the actuality of the secularization that has taken place despite them.

One of the most important consequences of this is that the state no longer serves as an enforcement agency on behalf of the previously dominant religious institution. Indeed, this is one of the major tenets in the political doctrine of the separation of state and Church, both in its American and French versions (whatever their other differences may be), and it is equally strongly expressed in the various doctrines of religious toleration and liberty even where these are not legitimated in terms of the separation of state and Church, as in England, Germany, or the Scandinavian countries. The state now takes on a role *vis-à-vis* the competing religious groups that is strikingly reminiscent of its role in *laissez-faire* capitalism – basically, that of impartial guardian of order between independent and uncoerced competitors. As we shall see in a moment, this analogy between economic and religious 'free enterprise' is far from accidental.

Of course, there are differences in the specific attitude taken by the state towards religion in different national societies. But if one keeps in mind the basic similarity of the cessation of coercion these differences appear as less than decisive. Thus there are obvious differences between the American situation, in which the state is most benign to religion and in which the different religious groups profit equally from the fiscal bonanza guaranteed to them by the tax exemption laws, and the situation in Communist Europe, in which the state, for its own ideological reasons, is hostile to religion in both theory and practice. It is important to keep in mind, though, that both these situations, if they are compared with traditional 'Christian societies', are similar to the extent that the Churches can no longer call upon the political arm to enforce their claims of allegiance. In both these situations the Churches are 'on their own' in having to enlist the voluntary adherence of their respective clienteles, though of course the American state facilitates their endeavour in the same measure as the Communist state tries to hinder them. Equally interesting is the failure of attempts to replicate the traditional coercive support of religion by the state under conditions of modernization. Contemporary Spain and Israel serve as interesting examples of such attempts, it being safe to say that in both cases the attempts are in process of failing. We would argue that the only chance of success in these countries would lie in the reversal of the modernization process, which would entail their remaking into pre-industrial societies – a goal as close to the impossible as anything in the realm of history.

The dynamics behind this are far from mysterious. Their roots are in the processes of rationalization released by modernization (that is, by the establishment of, first, a capitalist, then an industrial socio-economic order) in society at large and in the political institutions in particular.[5] The afore-mentioned 'liberated territory' of secularized sectors of society is so centrally 'located', in and around the capitalistic-industrial economy, that any attempt to 'reconquer' it in the name of religio-political traditionalism

endangers the continued functioning of this economy. A modern
industrial society requires the presence of large cadres of
scientific and technological personnel, whose training and ongoing social organization presupposes a high degree of rationalization, not only on the level of infrastructure but also on that
of consciousness. Any attempts at traditionalistic *reconquista*
thus threaten to dismantle the rational foundations of modern
society. Furthermore, the secularizing potency of capitalistic-
industrial rationalization is not only self-perpetuating but self-
aggrandizing. As the capitalistic industrial complex expands, so
do the social strata dominated by its rationales, and it becomes ever
more difficult to establish traditional controls over them. Since
the expansion of the same complex is international (today just
about world-wide), it becomes increasingly difficult to isolate any
particular national society from its rationalizing effects without
at the same time keeping that society in a condition of economic
backwardness. The impact of modern mass communications and
mass transportation (both nicely concentrated in the phenomenon of tourism) on contemporary Spain may serve as an illustration. As the modern state is increasingly occupied with the
political and legal requirements of the gigantic economic machinery of industrial production, it must gear its own structure
and ideology to this end. On the level of structure, this means
above all the establishment of highly rational bureaucracies; on
the level of ideology, it means the maintenance of legitimations
that are adequate for such bureaucracies. Thus, inevitably, there
develops an affinity, both in structure and in 'spirit', between the
economic and the political spheres. Secularization then passes
from the economic to the political sphere in a near-inexorable
process of 'diffusion'. The religious legitimations of the state are
then either liquidated altogether, or remain as rhetorical orna-
mentations devoid of social reality. It may be added that, given
an advanced state of industrialization, it seems of little consequence *in this respect* whether the rationalization of the political
order takes place under capitalist or socialist, democratic or
authoritarian auspices. The decisive variable for secularization
does not seem to be institutionalization of particular property

relations, nor the specifics of different constitutional systems, but rather the process of rationalization that is the prerequisite for *any* industrial society of the modern type.

While the presence of religion within modern political institutions is, typically, a matter of ideological rhetorics, this cannot be said about the opposite 'pole'. In the sphere of the family and of social relationships closely linked to it, religion continues to have considerable 'reality' potential, that is, continues to be relevant in terms of the motives and self-interpretations of people in this sphere of everyday social activity. The symbolic liaison between religion and the family is, of course, of ancient lineage indeed, grounded in the very antiquity of kinship institutions as such. The continuation of this liaison may then, in certain cases, be simply looked upon as an institutional 'survival'. More interesting, though, is the reappearance of the religious legitimation of the family even in highly secularized strata, as for instance in the contemporary American middle classes.[6] In these instances religion manifests itself in its peculiarly modern form, that is, as a legitimating complex voluntarily adopted by an uncoerced clientele. As such, it is located in the private sphere of everyday social life and is marked by the very peculiar traits of this sphere in modern society.[7] One of the essential traits is that of 'individualization'. This means that privatized religion is a matter of the 'choice' or 'preference' of the individual or the nuclear family, *ipso facto* lacking in common, binding quality. Such private religiosity, however 'real' it may be to the individuals who adopt it, cannot any longer fulfil the classical task of religion, that of constructing a common world within which all of social life receives ultimate meaning binding on everybody. Instead, this religiosity is limited to specific enclaves of social life that may be effectively segregated from the secularized sectors of modern society. The values pertaining to private religiosity are, typically, irrelevant to institutional contexts other than the private sphere. For example, a businessman or politician may faithfully adhere to the religiously legitimated norms of family life, while at the same time conducting his activities in the public sphere without any reference to religious values of any kind. It is not difficult to see that such segregation of religion within the private sphere is quite 'functional' for the maintenance of the highly rationalized order of modern economic and political institutions. The fact that this privatization of the religious tradition poses a problem for the theoreticians of the institutions embodying this tradition need not concern us at the moment.

The over-all effect of the afore-mentioned 'polarization' is very curious. Religion manifests itself as public rhetoric and private virtue. In other words, in so far as religion is common it lacks 'reality', and in so far as it is 'real' it lacks commonality. This situation represents a severe rupture of the traditional task of religion, which was precisely the establishment of an integrated set of definitions of reality that could serve as a common universe of meaning for the members of a society. The world-building potency of religion is thus restricted to the construction of subworlds, of fragmented universes of meaning, the plausibility structure of which may in some cases be no larger than the nuclear family. Since the modern family is notoriously fragile as an institution (a trait it shares with all other formations of the private sphere), this means that religion resting on this kind of plausibility structure is of necessity a tenuous construction. Put simply, a 'religious preference' can be abandoned as readily as it was first adopted. This tenuousness can (indeed must) be mitigated by seeking more broadly based plausibility structures. Typically, these are the Churches or other wider religious groupings. By the very nature of their social character as voluntary associations 'located' primarily in the private sphere, however, such Churches can only augment the strength and durability of the required plausibility structures to a limited extent.

The 'polarization' of religion brought about by secularization, and the concomitant loss of commonality and/or 'reality', can also be described by saying that secularization *ipso facto* leads to a pluralistic situation. The term 'pluralism', to be sure, has usually been applied only to those cases (of which the American one is prototypical) in which different religious groups are tolerated by the state and engage in free competition with each other. There is little point to arguments over terminology and there is nothing wrong with this limited use of the term. If, however, one looks at the underlying social forces producing even this limited kind of pluralism, the deeper linkage between secularization and pluralism becomes apparent. One may then say that, as we have seen, secularization brings about a demonopolization of religious traditions and thus, *ipso facto*, leads to a pluralistic situation.

Through most of human history religious establishments have existed as monopolies in society – monopolies, that is, in the ultimate legitimation of individual and collective life. Religious institutions really were *institutions* properly speaking, that is, regulatory agencies for both thought and action. The world as defined by the religious institution in question was *the* world, maintained not just by the mundane powers of the society and their instruments of social control, but much more fundamentally maintained by the 'common sense' of the members of that society. To step outside the world as religiously defined was to step into a chaotic darkness, into anomy, possibly into madness. This did not necessarily mean that the monopolistic religious institutions were externally tyrannical in the enforcement of their definitions of reality. Indeed, religious 'tyranny' in this sense has been mainly the prerogative of the religious traditions derived from the Biblical orbit, is generally absent in the orbit of the great religions of eastern Asia. But the fact that Hinduism, for instance, did not produce an inquisition does not mean that it did not establish an effective monopoly of reality-definition and legitimation in classical Indian society. Rival definitions of reality were either absorbed into the Hindu system socially and ideationally (by becoming a caste or a sect *within* Hinduism), or defined in such a way that they remained religiously irrelevant for those within the system (thus all non-Hindus were ritually impure to begin with, which allowed their 'mad' ideas to be neutralized in the consciousness of the Hindu as natural expressions of their existential impurity). Where groups embodying rival definitions of reality were physically present on the territory of the system, they were effectively segregated from Hindu society by the same ritual taboos and thus prevented from 'contaminating' the world as defined by Hinduism (the Zoroastrian Parsis are a good illustration). The great crisis of Hinduism came when India was conquered by foreigners who could no longer be dealt with in this manner, but even under Muslim and Christian rule Hindu society succeeded for a long time in using the traditional methods of self-encapsulation to prevent conquest from being followed by inner disintegration. Only with the modernization of India in very recent times is it possible to observe the emergence of genuine pluralism, expressed politically by the self-definition of independent India as a secular state.

In the West it was the concept and the social reality of Christendom that expressed the religious monopoly. In contrast with Hinduism, Christendom freely employed military violence against the unbelievers both outside its gate (notably in the Crusades against Islam) and inside them (as in the persecutions of heretics and Jews). The monopolistic character of Christendom was not vitiated by the fact that *two* institutions, namely Church and empire, struggled for the honour of being its principal embodiment. Both institutions represented the *same* religious world. The struggle between them had more the character of an intramural conflict rather than a confrontation with outside rivals – if the analogy be permitted, more like a fight between two factions within a corporation than like competition *between* corporations. All the same, just as we have previously argued that the peculiar institution of the Christian Church carried within it a secularizing potential, we would also say that it facilitated the later establishment of a genuinely pluralistic situation. The pluralistic potential was realized in the wake of the Wars of Religion. When the settlement of these wars established the principle of *cuius regio eius religio*, it did not thereby, of course, set up a pluralistic situation. On the contrary, the Protestants were as violent in their efforts to exercise monopolistic control over their territories as the Catholics. But once the unity of Christendom was effectively broken, a process was set in motion that made further fragmentations much easier of accomplishment and which eventually, for practical rather than ideological reasons, led to an ever-widening toleration of religious deviance both in the Protestant and Catholic territories. This is not the place to go into the historical details of this process. For well-known historical reasons the pluralizing process first came to fruition in America, resulting in the establishment of a system of mutually tolerant denominations that has persisted to this day. The denomination of the American type has, indeed, been defined as a Church that has had to come to terms with the permanent presence and competition of other Churches within its own territory.[8]

In the American type of denominationalism (which, unlike other American institutions, has shown itself as an exportable product of international attractiveness), different religious groups, all with the same legal status, compete *with each other*. Pluralism, however, is not limited to this type of intrareligious competition. As a result of secularization religious groups are also compelled to compete with various *non*-religious rivals in the business of defining the world, some of them highly organized (such as various ideological movements of revolution or nationalism), others much more diffused institutionally (such as the modern value systems of 'individualism' or sexual emancipation). Thus it is not only in national societies with an American-type denominational system that one may speak of pluralism, but anywhere where religious ex-monopolies are forced to deal with legally tolerated and socially powerful rivals in the definition of reality. In this way French Catholicism, for example, has been compelled into pluralistic competition *not* by the relatively insignificant Protestant minority *but* by the massive presence of non-religious rivals in various strata of the society (highly organized in the working-class movements, diffuse in the 'secularism' of the middle classes). It should not surprise us that, consequently, 'American' ideas of religious liberty and of the general social-ethical stance of organized religion should have found an echo in places that never developed an American-type denominational system. This is hardly to be ascribed to the missionary success of American Protestant liberalism, but rather to the global dynamics of pluralism as a phenomenon grounded in the infrastructure of modern societies.

The key characteristic of all pluralistic situations, whatever the details of their historical background, is that the religious ex-monopolies can no longer take for granted the allegiance of their client populations. Allegiance is voluntary and thus, by definition, less than certain. As a result, the religious tradition, which previously could be authoritatively imposed, now has to be *marketed*. It must be 'sold' to a clientele that is no longer constrained to 'buy'. The pluralistic situation is, above all, a *market situation*. In it, the religious institutions become marketing agencies and the religious traditions become consumer commodities. And at any rate a good deal of religious activity in this situation comes to be dominated by the logic of market economics.

It is not difficult to see that this situation will have far-reaching consequences for the social structure of the various religious groups. What happens here, quite simply, is that the religious groups are transformed from monopolies to competitive marketing agencies. Previously, the religious groups were organized as befits an institution exercising exclusive control over a population of retainers. Now, the religious groups must organize themselves in such a way as to woo a population of consumers, in competition with other groups having the same purpose. All at once, the question of 'results' becomes important. In the monopolistic situation the socio-religious structures are under no pressure to produce 'results' – the situation itself predefines the 'results'. Medieval France, for instance, was Catholic by definition. Contemporary France, however, can be so defined only in the teeth of overwhelmingly contrary evidence. It has become, indeed, a *pays de mission*. Consequently, the Catholic Church must raise the question of its own social structure, precisely in order to make possible the achievement of missionary 'results'. The confrontation with this question accounts in large measure for the turmoil through which French Catholicism has passed in recent years.[9]

The pressure to achieve 'results' in a competitive situation entails a rationalization of the socio-religious structures. However these may be legitimated by the theologians, the men charged with the mundane welfare of the various religious groups must see to it that the structures permit the rational execution of the groups' 'mission'. As in other institutional spheres of modern society, such structural rationalization expresses itself primarily in the phenomenon of bureaucracy.[10]

The spread of bureaucratic structures through the religious institutions has the consequence that these, irrespective of their various theological traditions, increasingly resemble each other sociologically. The traditional terminology pertaining to matters of 'polity' usually obfuscates this fact. Thus a certain position, A, may carry out the same bureaucratic functions in two different religious groups, but it may be legitimated by theological formula B in one group and by formula C in the other, and indeed the two theological legitimations may be directly contradictory without affecting the functionality of the position in question. For instance, the control over investment funds may be in the charge of a bishop in one group and of the chairman of a laymen's committee in another, yet the actual bureaucratic activities necessitated by this position will have little if any connection with the traditional legitimations of the episcopate or of lay authority. To be sure, there are different models or *Leitbilder* of bureaucracy involved in this process. Thus European Protestant Churches, with long experience in state-Church situations, will tend towards political models of bureaucracy, while American Protestantism tends to emulate the bureaucratic structures of economic corporations. The central administration of the Catholic Church, on the other hand, has its own bureaucratic tradition, which so far has shown itself highly resistant to modernizing modifications. But the demands of rationality are very similar in all these cases and exercise similarly strong pressure on the respective socio-religious structures.

The contemporary situation of religion is thus characterized by a progressive bureaucratization of the religious institutions. Both their internal and their external social relations are marked by this process. Internally, the religious institutions are not only administered bureaucratically, but their day-to-day operations are dominated by the typical problems and 'logic' of bureaucracy.

Externally, the religious institutions deal with other social institutions as well as with each other through the typical forms of bureaucratic interaction. 'Public relations' with the consumer clientele, 'lobbying' with the government, 'fund raising' with both governmental and private agencies, multifaceted involvements with the secular economy (particularly through investment) – in all these aspects of their 'mission' the religious institutions are compelled to seek 'results' by methods that are, of necessity, very similar to those employed by other bureaucratic structures with similar problems. Very importantly, the same bureaucratic 'logic' applies to the dealings of the several religious institutions with each other.

Bureaucracies demand specific types of personnel. This personnel is specific not only in terms of its functions and requisite skills, but also in terms of its psychological characteristics. Bureaucratic institutions both *select* and *form* the personnel types they require for their operation.[11] This means that similar types of leadership emerge in the several religious institutions, irrespective of the traditional patterns in this matter. The requirements of bureaucracy override such traditional differentiations of religious leadership as 'prophet' versus 'priest', 'scholar' versus 'saint', and so forth. Thus it does not matter very much whether a certain bureaucratic functionary comes out of a Protestant tradition of 'prophetic' ministry or a Catholic tradition of 'priestly' one – in either case, he must above all adapt himself to the requirements of his bureaucratic role. Where possible, the traditional formulas will be retained to legitimate the new social-psychological types; where this is no longer possible, they will have to be modified in order to permit such legitimation. For example, theological scholarship was traditionally central to the role of the Protestant minister; it has become increasingly irrelevant to the roles of the ministry both in 'wholesale' (bureaucratic administration) and 'retail' (local marketing) operations; Protestant educational institutions for the ministry have been accordingly modified, with concomitant modifications in their legitimating rationales.[12] The social-psychological type emerging in the leadership of the bureaucratized religious institutions is, naturally, similar to the bureaucratic personality in other institutional contexts – activist, pragmatically oriented, not given to administratively irrelevant reflection, skilled in inter-personal relations, 'dynamic' and conservative at the same time, and so forth. The individuals conforming to this type in the different religious institutions speak the same language and, nat-urally, understand each other and each other's problems. In other words, the bureaucratization of the religious institutions lays a social-psychological foundation for 'ecumenicity' – an important fact to understand, we would contend.

'Ecumenicity', however, in the sense of an increasingly friendly collaboration between the different groups engaged in the religious market, is demanded by the pluralistic situation as a whole, not just by the social-psychological affinities of religio-bureaucratic personnel. These affinities ensure, if nothing else, that religious rivals are regarded not so much as 'the enemy' but as fellows with similar problems. This, obviously, makes col-laboration easier. But the necessity to collaborate is given by the need to rationalize competition itself in the pluralistic situation. The competitive market is established once it has become impos-sible to utilize the political machinery of the society for the elim-ination of religious rivals. The forces of this market then tend towards a system of free competition very similar to that of *laissez-faire* capitalism. Such a system, however, requires further rationalization as it develops. Free competition between the different marketing agencies, without any restraints imposed from without or agreed upon by these agencies themselves, becomes irrational at the point where the cost of such com-petition begins to jeopardize the gains to be derived from it. This cost may, first of all, be political and in terms of 'public image'. Thus it may be easier to extract favours from a religiously neutral government by different Churches acting in concert than by trying to undercut each other. Also, overly savage competition for consumer patronage may be self-defeating in as much as it may have the effect of alienating various classes of potential 'cus-tomers' from the religious market altogether. But untrammelled competition also tends to become irrational, that is, too costly, in purely economic terms. The marketing of any commodity, material or otherwise, to a modern mass public is an exceedingly complex and expensive operation. Thus any new venture on the part of the Churches (particularly what is called 'Church expansion in America) necessitates the expenditure of substantial capital. The bureaucrats in charge of these operations must calculate rationally, which in turn forces them to reduce the risks as much as possible. The training of religious personnel, the construction and upkeep of religious edifices, the output of promotional materials, the rising overhead of bureaucratic administration – all these entail vast sums of money, for the rational use of which the religious bureaucrats are responsible. The responsibility increases to the extent that the supply of funds for these purposes is subject to exigency. This may be because the sources of income have become uncertain – the 'giving' habits of uncoerced clients and/or of governmental funding agencies may be hard to predict accurately, thus introducing elements of risk into the calculations. Or it may be because of inflation in the economy at large, making all expenditures a more risky undertaking (an important element in all 'Church expansion' programmes in America). One obvious way of reducing risks is to come to various kinds of understanding with one's competitors – to 'fix prices' – that is, to rationalize competition by means of cartelization.

An excellent illustration of what this means is the development of 'comity' in American Protestantism.[13] The term (now fallen into disuse) refers to agreements between different denominations as to the territories to be allocated to their respective 'expansion' programmes. Such allocation (now called by more explicitly bureaucratic terminology, largely derived from the field of community planning) is rationalized to a high degree, routinely involves the use of census data, real-estate and demographic projections, as well as survey data gathered by the research departments of the denominational bureaucracies themselves. Thus it is not only as the outcome of political negotiations, but on the basis of highly rational, objective information that a decision to allocate a territory (say, a new suburban development) to a particular denomination is made. The growth of interdenominational agencies in American Protestantism, both on the local and regional level (that is, the so-called 'conciliar' movement), is directly related to these bureaucratic necessities and (rhetorics apart) the largest portion of their activities continues to be geared to the same. Any drastic change in this pattern would inevitably lead to severe disturbances in the economies of the several denominations.

Cartelization, here as elsewhere in competitive market situations, has two facets: the number of competing units is reduced through mergers; and the remaining units organize the market by means of mutual agreements. 'Ecumenicity', in the contemporary situation, is, of course, characterized by both of these two facets. At any rate within Protestantism, Churches have merged at an increasing rate and negotiations looking forward to further mergers are continuing apace. Both within and beyond Protestantism, there has been increasing consultation and collaboration between the large bodies 'surviving' the merger process. It is important to see that this process of cartelization does *not* tend towards the re-establishment of a monopoly situation – in other words, the notion of an eventual 'world church' is very unlikely to be realized empirically. Rather, the tendency is clearly oligopolistic, with mergers in prospect only to the extent that these are functional in terms of rationalizing competition. To go beyond this extent, quite apart from the strain this would put on the theological legitimations, would actually be irrational in terms of the institutional interests of the several religious bureaucracies. Nor is it easily imaginable that this would meet consumer demand (which, ironically, is frequently more traditional in its denominational loyalties than the thinking of the religious bureaucrats).

The pluralistic situation thus entails a network of bureaucratic structures, engaged in rational dealings with the society at large and with each other. The pluralistic situation, in as much as it tends towards cartelization, tends towards 'ecumenicity' in its social, political and economic dynamics. The quotation marks should indicate that this tendency need not be related *a priori* to any particular theological conceptions about the term. It is very likely that something like the present-day ecumenical movement would have resulted from the pluralistic situation in any case, even if there had not been the particular theological developments now used to legitimate it. Indeed, it seems plausible, to the sociologist at any rate, to see the theological developments as consequences rather than cause of the pluralistic infrastructure, without thereby denying their capacity to 'act back' upon that infrastructure. It goes without saying, of course, that seeing the matter in this way does not in the least impugn the sincerity of the theological motives of anyone engaged in the ecumenical movement. 'Conspiracy theories' are rarely convincing when it comes to large-scale social phenomena, but they are particularly unsatisfying when the phenomena have a religious character.

The effects of the pluralistic situation are not limited to the social-structural aspects of religion. They also extend to the religious contents, that is, to the product of the religious marketing agencies. It should not be difficult to see why this should be so, in view of the preceding discussion of structural changes. As long as religious institutions occupied a monopoly position in society, their contents could be determined in accordance with whatever theological lore seemed plausible and/or convenient to the religious leadership. This does not mean, of course, that the leadership and its theological decisions were immune to forces originating in the larger society, for instance within the power centres of the latter. Religion has always been susceptible to highly mundane influences, extending even to its most rarefied theoretical constructions. The pluralistic situation, however, introduces a novel form of mundane influences, probably more potent in modifying religious contents than such older forms as the wishes of kings or the vested interests of classes – the dynamics of consumer preference.

To repeat, the crucial sociological and social-psychological characteristic of the pluralistic situation is that religion can no longer be imposed but must be marketed. It is impossible, almost *a priori*, to market a commodity to a population of uncoerced consumers without taking their wishes concerning the commodity into consideration. To be sure, the religious institutions can still count on traditional ties holding back certain groups of the population from too drastic liberty in religious choice – in terms of the market, there still is strong 'product loyalty' among certain groups of 'old customers'. Furthermore, the religious institutions can to a certain extent restrain disaffection among the same groups by means of their own promotional activities. All the same, the basic necessity of taking on a soliciting stance *vis-à-vis* a public means that consumer controls over the product being marketed are introduced.

This means, furthermore, that a dynamic element is introduced into the situation, a principle of changeability if not change, that is intrinsically inimical to religious traditionalism. In other words, in this situation it becomes increasingly difficult to maintain the religious traditions as unchanging verity. Instead, the dynamics of consumer preference is introduced into the religious sphere. Religious contents become subjects of 'fashion'. This need not necessarily imply that there will be rapid change or that the principle of unchangeability will be no surrendered theologically, but the *possibility* of change is introduced into the situation once and for all. Sooner or later, the chances are that the possibility will be realized and that the possibility will eventually be legitimated on the level of theological theorizing. This is obviously easier to admit for some religious groups than for others (for instance, for the Protestants than for the Catholics), but no group can escape this effect completely.

The dynamics of consumer preference does not, in itself, determine the substantive contents – it simply posits that, in principle, they are susceptible to change, without determining the direction of change. However, there are some other factors in the contemporary situation that have substantive influence on the character of this change. In so far as the world of the consumers in question is secularized, their preference will reflect this. That is, they will prefer religious products that can be made consonant with secularized consciousness over those that cannot. This will, of course, vary with the strata that serve as clienteles for different religious institutions. Consumer demand in upper-middle-class suburbia in America, for instance, is different in this respect from consumer demand in the rural South. Given the variability in the degree of secularization of different strata, the secularizing influence of these strata as religious consumers will vary. But in as much as secularization is a global trend, there is a global tendency for religious contents to be modified in a secularizing direction. In the extreme cases (as in liberal Protestantism and Judaism) this may lead to the deliberate excision of all or nearly all 'supernatural' elements from the religious tradition, and a legitimation of the continued existence of the institution that once embodied the tradition in purely secular terms. In other cases it may just mean that the 'supernatural' elements are de-emphasized or pushed into the background, while the institution is 'sold' under the label of values congenial to secularized consciousness. For example, the Catholic Church is obviously less ready to 'de-mythologize' its contents than most of its Protestant competitors, but *both* traditional Catholicism *and* 'progressive' Protestantism can be effectively advertised as strengthening the moral fibre of the nation or as supplying various psychological benefits ('peace of mind' and the like).

Another substantive influence comes from the institutional 'location' of religion in contemporary society. Since the socially significant 'relevance' of religion is primarily in the private sphere, consumer preference reflects the 'needs' of this sphere. This means that religion can more easily be marketed if it can be shown to be 'relevant' to private life than if it is advertised as entailing specific applications to the large public institutions. This is particularly important for the moral and therapeutic functions of religion. As a result, the religious institutions have accommodated themselves to the moral and therapeutic 'needs' of the individual in his private life. This manifests itself in the prominence given to private problems in the activity and promotion of contemporary religious institutions – the emphasis on family and neighbourhood as well as on the psychological 'needs' of the private individual. It is in these areas that religion continues to be 'relevant' even in highly secularized strata, while the application of religious perspectives to political and economic problems is widely deemed 'irrelevant' in the same strata. This, incidentally, helps to explain why the Churches have had relatively little influence on the economic and political views of even their own members, while continuing to be cherished by the latter in their existence as private individuals.

The pluralistic situation, then, has, not surprisingly, coincided with a new emphasis on the laity in the religious institutions. The 'age of the laity', as defined by a number of theologians, is grounded in the character of this laity as a population of consumers. In other words, the theological propositions about the role of the laity may be understood as *post hoc* legitimations of developments rooted in the infrastructure of the contemporary religious market. Again, some religious traditions have been easier to modify in this direction than others. Thus Protestants in the free church tradition have been able to legitimate the dominance of consumer demand and controls in terms of venerable theological propositions (despite the fact that, of course, these propositions originally referred to an entirely different situation – the Puritan covenant, for instance, hardly referred to a consumers' cooperative). It is all the more interesting to see how the same 'rediscovery of the laity' has been taking place in religious traditions previously bereft of such legitimations, as even within Catholicism.[14]

Two other effects of consumer controls over religious contents are standardization and marginal differentiation – once more replications of the general dynamics of a free market. In so far as the religious 'needs' of certain strata of clients or potential clients are similar, the religious institutions catering to these 'needs' will tend to standardize their products accordingly. For example, all religious institutions oriented towards the upper-middle-class market in America will be under pressure to secularize and to psychologize their products – otherwise, the chances of these being 'bought' diminish drastically. Thus even the Catholic priest in suburbia is much less likely to talk about Fatima than to engage in a 'dialogue' with some available psychiatrist on 'religion and mental health'. His Protestant and Jewish colleagues, of course, are likely to have legitimated their whole operations as some kind of family psychotherapy long ago. This standardization of religious contents, brought about by consumer pressures, tends to de-emphasize traditional confessional cleavages. As a result, it facilitates the cartelization necessitated by the structural features of the pluralistic situation. Group *A* may merge or 'fix prices' with group *B* simply as a result of the pragmatic problems faced by the two bureaucracies in question, but the operation is easier to accomplish when, in fact, contents *A* and *B* have become close to being indistinguishable.

The pluralistic situation, however, has engendered not only the 'age of ecumenicity' but also, apparently in contradiction to it, the 'age of rediscovery of confessional heritages'. This has often been observed and simply noted as some sort of 'countervailing movement', welcomed or deplored as the case may be.[15] It is important to see, we would contend, that the renewed emphasis on denominational identities (specifically, those identities that survive the cartelization process) is actually part of the same process of the rationalization of competition. The 'countervailing movement' is brought about by the need for marginal differentiation in an over-all situation of standardization. Put simply, if group *A* decides *not* to merge with group *B,* despite the fact that their products have become highly standardized, something must be done to enable consumers to distinguish between the two products and to be able to make a choice between them. Emphasizing the 'confessional heritage' of each group is one obvious way of doing this. It may happen that this will actually arrest or even reverse the process of standardization. It may also happen (probably more frequently) that the differentiation is one of 'packaging' only – inside the package there may still be the same old standardized product. In either case, it is likely that marginal differentiation will go only as far as is necessitated by the dynamics of consumer demand in any particular market. This will vary, then, not so much in accordance with specific confessional traditions but rather with the variations of consumer 'needs' in terms of general social stratification. The 'rediscovery of confessional heritages', therefore, is not very aptly described as a 'countervailing movement' to 'ecumenicity', but is rather to be understood as a structurally required counterpart to the latter. The differentiation of religious products in these terms will then have a social-psychological correlate. That is, once group A has been 'profiled' in terms of its 'rediscovered' tradition, representatives of group A will have to define themselves as standing in this tradition as they confront the representatives of other groups. This goes far to explain the dynamics of identification and self-identification in the 'who's who' of contemporary ecumenism – by definition, every participant in the latter must be something – all the social-psychological pressures of the situation then push him towards becoming what he is supposed to be, namely a representative of the religious tradition to which he has been assigned.

It is clear that all this creates serious problems for the theorists of the various religious institutions – that is, it creates a problem of theological legitimation. This we will look at a little more closely in the following chapter. But there is an underlying social-psychological process that must be understood – namely, a change in the 'location' of religion within consciousness.[16]

As we have seen much earlier, the objectivity (that is, objective reality) of religious worlds is constructed and maintained through empirically available social processes. Any particular religious world will present itself to consciousness as reality only to the extent that its appropriate plausibility structure is kept in existence. If the plausibility structure is massive and durable, the religious world maintained thereby will be massively and durably real in consciousness. In the optimal case, the religious world will then be simply taken for granted. However, as the plausibility structure is weakened, so will the subjective reality of the religious world in question. Uncertainty makes its appearance. What was previously taken for granted as self-evident reality may now only be reached by a deliberate effort, an act of 'faith', which by definition will have to overcome doubts that keep on lurking in the background. In a further disintegration of the plausibility structure, the old religious contents can only be maintained in consciousness as 'opinions' or 'feelings' – or, as the American phrase aptly puts it, as a 'religious preference'. This entails a shift in the 'location' of these contents in consciousness. They 'percolate up', as it were, from the levels of consciousness that contain the fundamental 'truths' on which at least all 'sane' men will agree to the levels on which various 'subjective' views are held – views on which intelligent people readily disagree and of which one is not altogether sure oneself.

That something of this order has been happening to religion in contemporary consciousness is widely recognized. Indeed, the contemporary period is widely designated as an 'age of scepticism'. What is not widely recognized, however, is that this fact is not due to some mysterious metamorphosis of consciousness in and of itself, but is rather to be explained in terms of empirically available social developments. To wit, the pluralistic situation described above *ipso facto* plunges religion into a crisis of credibility.

It does so, first of all, by virtue of its linkage with secularization. As we have seen, the two global processes of pluralization and secularization are closely linked. However, there would also be a crisis in credibility brought on by pluralism as a *social-structural* phenomenon, quite apart from its linkage with the 'carriers' of secularization. The pluralistic situation, in de-monopolizing religion, makes it ever more difficult to maintain or to construct anew viable plausibility structures for religion. The plausibility structures lose massivity because they can no longer enlist the society as a whole to serve for the purpose of social confirmation. Put simply, there are always 'all those others' that refuse to confirm the religious world in question. Put simply in a different way, it becomes increasingly difficult for the 'inhabitants' of any particular religious world to remain *entre nous* in contemporary society. Disconfirming others (not just individuals, but entire strata) can no longer be safely kept away from 'one's own'. Furthermore the plausibility structures lose the appearance of durability as a result of the afore-mentioned dynamics of consumer culture. As religious contents become susceptible to 'fashion' it becomes increasingly difficult to maintain them as unchangeable verities. These processes, to repeat, are not understood if one views them only as phenomena of consciousness –

rather, they must be understood as grounded in the specific infrastructure established by modern industrial society. One may say, with only some exaggeration, that economic data or industrial productivity or capital expansion can predict the religious crisis of credibility in a particular society more easily than data derived from the 'history of ideas' of that society.

The pluralistic situation multiplies the number of plausibility structures competing with each other. *Ipso facto*, it relativizes their religious contents. More specifically, the religious contents are 'de-objectivated', that is, deprived of their status as taken-for-granted, objective reality in consciousness. They become 'subjectivized' in a double sense: their 'reality' becomes a 'private' affair of individuals, that is, loses the quality of self-evident intersubjective plausibility – thus one 'cannot really talk' about religion any more. And their 'reality', in so far as it is still maintained by the individual, is apprehended as being rooted within the consciousness of the individual rather than in any facticities of the external world – religion no longer refers to the cosmos or to history, but to individual *Existenz* or psychology.

On the level of theorizing, this phenomenon serves to explain the current linkage of theology with the conceptual machineries of existentialism and psychologism. These conceptual machineries are, indeed, 'empirically adequate' to the extent that they accurately reflect the 'location' of religion in contemporary consciousness, which they merely serve to legitimate theoretically. It is important to understand that these legitimations are grounded in pretheoretical phenomena of consciousness, which are grounded in turn in the infrastructure of contemporary society. The individual in fact 'discovers' religion within his own subjective consciousness, somewhere 'deep down' within himself – the existentialist or Freudian theoretician then merely explicates this 'discovery' on the level of theory. Once more, we would contend, we may predict these phenomena more accurately by means of economic data than by any 'data' on, say, the workings of the 'unconscious'. Indeed, the emergence of the 'unconscious' itself may be analysed in terms of specific structural developments of modern industrial society.[17]

In this way the demonopolization of religion is a social-structural as well as a social-psychological process. Religion no longer legitimates 'the world'. Rather, different religious groups seek, by different means, to maintain their particular subworlds in the face of a plurality of competing subworlds. Concomitantly, this plurality of religious legitimations is internalized in consciousness as a plurality of possibilities between which one may choose. *Ipso facto*, any particular choice is relativized and less than certain. What certainty there is must be dredged up from within the subjective consciousness of the individual, since it can no longer be derived from the external, socially shared and taken-for-granted world. This 'dredging up' can then be legitimated as a 'discovery' of some alleged existential or psychological data. The religious traditions have lost their character as overarching symbols for the society at large, which must find its integrating symbolism elsewhere. Those who continue to adhere to the world as defined by the religious traditions then find themselves in the position of cognitive minorities – a status that has social-psychological as well as theoretical problems.

The pluralistic situation presents the religious institutions with two ideal-typical options. They can either accommodate themselves to the situation, play the pluralistic game of religious free enterprise, and come to terms as best they can with the plausibility problem by modifying their product in accordance with consumer demands. Or they can refuse to accommodate themselves, entrench themselves behind whatever socio-religious structures they can maintain or construct, and continue to profess the old objectives as much as possible as if nothing had happened. Obviously there are various intermediate possibilities between these two ideal-typical options, with varying degrees of accommodation and intransigence. Both ideal-typical options have problems on the level of theory as well as on the level of 'social engineering'. These problems *together* constitute the 'crisis of theology' and the 'crisis of the Church' in contemporary society. This we shall turn to next.

Secularization and the Problem of Legitimation

Enough has been said in the preceding pages to make clear that our approach is neither 'idealistic' nor 'materialistic', as regards the relationship between theory and *praxis* in religious phenomena. Indeed, in looking at any particular historical situation of religion it is very largely a matter of convenience (more precisely, a question of the specific cognitive goal of the inquiry) as to which of the two spheres one begins with. Depending on the starting point, one may then be able to show how a particular theoretical constellation results from a certain practical infrastructure, or conversely how a particular social structure is the result of certain movements in the realm of ideas. Thus, in the foregoing analyses, it is just as possible to say that pluralism produces secularization as it is to say that secularization produces pluralism. This is not due, we daresay, to any sloppiness in thinking or ambiguity of terms, but rather to the intrinsic dialecticity of the phenomena under scrutiny, and indeed of socio-historical phenomena in general. If, then, we conclude our argument with a look at certain elements of religious theorizing, we thereby intend to imply *neither* that these elements are 'nothing but' the effect of the previously analysed social-structural processes *nor* that they can finally be seen as the 'real' or 'underlying' forces in the situation. Put simply, this just happens to be a convenient place to bring our argument to an end.

The 'crisis of theology' in the contemporary religious situation is grounded in a crisis of plausibility that precedes any theorizing. That is, the plausibility of traditional religious definitions of reality is put in question in the minds of ordinary people with no knowledge of or even interest in theology. We have tried to show in the preceding chapter that this crisis of religion on the level of commonsense knowledge is not due to any mysterious metamorphosis of consciousness, but can rather be explained in terms of empirically available developments in the social structures and the social psychology of modern societies. As we have seen, the fundamental problem of the religious institutions is how to keep going in a milieu that no longer takes for granted their definitions of reality. We have also indicated that the two basic options open to them are those of accommodation and resistance to the massive impact of this milieu. It will be clear that both options engender both practical and theoretical difficulties. Both practically and theoretically, the difficulty of the accommodating posture lies in deciding the question, 'How far should one go?', of the resisting posture in knowing at any point, 'How strong are the defences?' The practical difficulties must be met by means of 'social engineering' – in the accommodating posture, reorganizing the institution in order to make it 'more relevant' to the modern world; in the resisting posture, maintaining or revamping the institution so as to serve as a viable plausibility structure for reality-definitions that are not confirmed by the larger society. Both options, of course, must be theoretically legitimated. It is precisely in this legitimation that the 'crisis of theology' is rooted.

To the extent that secularization and pluralism are today world-wide phenomena, the theological crisis is also world-wide, despite, of course, the vast differences in the religious contents that must be legitimated. Indeed, it makes sense to include in the same over-all crisis the difficulties faced by the legitimators of non-religious *Weltanschauungen*, particularly that of dogmatic Marxism. In a very real way, however, the Protestant development is prototypical, to the point where one can even say that quite possibly all other religious traditions in the modern situation may be predestined to go through variants of the Protestant experience. The reason for the prototypicality of Protestantism, of course, lies in the peculiar relationship of the latter to the genesis and inner character of the modern world, a matter we have discussed before. In the following pages, then, we shall concentrate on the unfolding 'crisis of theology' in Protestantism, though our interest is in a much broader phenomenon. If the drama of the modern era is the decline of religion, then Protestantism can aptly be described as its dress rehearsal.

As is well known, early Protestantism was no more ready than its Catholic antagonist to make concessions to secularizing thought or to accept the limitations of a pluralistic situation.[1] All three major branches of the Reformation – Lutheran, Anglican, and Calvinist – sought to set up facsimiles of Christendom in their respective territories. It can be argued that these lacked plausibility by comparison with their medieval model simply as a result of their diminished size and continual confrontation with contradictory definitions of the situation. But it took a good while before this reality-loss began to be reflected on the level of theological legitimation. Lutheran, Anglican, and Calvinist orthodoxies maintained themselves in plausibility structures that were kept as closed as the contingencies of the situation permitted – and frequently through methods that were as repressive as those of the Catholics. On the level of theological theorizing, Protestant orthodoxy went through two severe shocks prior to the nineteenth century. One was the shock of pietism, taking different forms in the three major Protestant groupings – pietism proper within Lutheranism, the Methodist movement originating within the Church of England, and a variety of revivalistic movements in the Calvinist camp (such as the first Great Awakening in New England at the time of Jonathan Edwards). Pietism constituted a shock to Protestant orthodoxy because it 'melted down' the dogmatic structures of the latter in various forms of emotionalism. It was thus de-objectivating or 'subjectivizing' (in the sense explicated in the preceding chapter), as nicely illustrated by Wesley's notion of the 'warmed heart'. The 'subjectivization' this entailed is of a double kind – subjective emotionality takes the place of objective dogma as a criterion of religious legitimacy, thus laying a foundation for the 'psychologization' of Christianity – and the same process relativizes the religious contents, since the 'heart' of one individual may say different things from the 'heart' of another. Pietism also threatened the Protestant effort to maintain micro-Christendoms by virtue of its pluralizing tendency. Beginning with the original *ecclesiola in ecclesia* of Spener and Zinzendorf, pietism in all its forms tended towards sectarianism both within and outside the traditional Churches.

The other shock was that of Enlightenment rationalism, felt throughout the Protestant world as an intense challenge to orthodoxy. Very probably this is to be seen as a logical (though, of course, unintended) consequence of the pietistic erosion of orthodoxy – and indeed, pietism and rationalism have shown considerable affinity ever since, down to the contemporary merging of the two in psychologism. Enlightenment rationalism in theological thought was an international movement, taking very similar forms irrespective of whether it appeared in a Lutheran, Anglican, or Calvinist context. An exemplary figure of the movement was Lessing.

It would take us far afield if we now pursued the question of the infrastructural aspects of these developments, important though this would be for a historical sociology of Protestantism. Suffice it to state axiomatically that, of course, these theological developments had their *Sitz im Leben* in broad processes affecting the societies in which Protestantism existed. Be these what they may, the real 'crisis' of Protestant orthodoxy came to the fore in the nineteenth century. And the main fruit of nineteenth-century Protestant theology was the emergence of a cohesive theological liberalism which, though short-lived as a historical phenomenon at least in its classical form, was of impressive theoretical scope. It affected all fields of theological thought – Biblical studies, Church history, ethics, systematic theology. In the first two areas, especially in Germany, Protestant liberalism brought about some of the most impressive achievements of modern historical scholarship. Albeit with vastly different conceptual tools, Protestant liberalism attained a theoretical synthesis that may well be compared with the Thomist one.

The 'father' of this liberal synthesis was Friedrich Schleiermacher and the main features of later liberal theology can already be clearly seen in his own thought.[2] There is the central emphasis on religious experience, understood as a 'feeling for the infinite', later as a 'feeling of absolute dependence'. All dogmatic formulations are relativized on this basis. All 'supernatural' elements in the Christian tradition are de-emphasized in favour of a 'natural' religion, in which both reason and the emotions will be satisfied. Religious history is understood in evolutionistic terms, with Christianity interpreted as the 'highest religion' because of its supposedly unique features. There is a romantic (and, in its roots, pietistic) fascination with the human figure of Jesus. There is an optimistic conception of Christian ethics as furnishing a set of positive values both for the individual and for culture, the latter aspect serving as the basis of what was aptly called *Kulturprotestantismus* – a liaison between Protestant liberalism and the liberal culture of the bourgeoisie that already indicates the infrastructural roots of the theological phenomenon.

In all of this should be noted the attitude of defensiveness *vis-à-vis* what are taken to be definitive truths of philosophy and science, that is of secular reason, outside the Christian sphere. In other words, the theological enterprise now takes place with constant regard for a reference group of secular intellectuals – precisely the 'cultured despisers' of religion to whom Schleiermacher addressed his famous lectures in 1799. *They*, rather than the sources of his own tradition, now serve the Protestant theologian as arbiters of cognitive acceptability. It is with *them* that the necessary intellectual compromises are 'negotiated'. This defensive attitude ('apologetic' in the modern sense of the word, as against the classical meaning of 'apologetics' in the Church) continued as a crucial characteristic of the 'liberal century' that followed Schleiermacher in Protestant theology. This theology can, indeed, be described as an immense bargaining process with secular thought – 'We'll give you the miracles of Jesus, but we'll keep his ethics'; 'You can have the virgin birth, but we'll hold on to the resurrection'; and so on. Figures like Kierkegaard, who were unwilling to follow these lines, remained marginal to the theological situation and only came into their own after the end of the 'Schleiermachian era'.

We cannot possibly try to discuss the development of Protestant liberal theology in its (often fascinating) historical details. We would only point to what, pretty much beyond doubt, can be regarded as the infrastructural foundation of Protestant liberalism – the period of capitalist triumphs in economy and technology, of Western expansion, and of bourgeois cultural dominance – in sum, the 'golden age' of bourgeois capitalism. This was a period of profound confidence in the cultural, political, and economic values of Western civilization, a confidence fully reflected in the optimistic *Weltanschauung* of Protestant liberalism. The compromises of the theologian, consequently, were not negotiated under duress, but in the confrontation with a secular culture deemed eminently attractive and praiseworthy, not just materially but in its values. Put crudely, it paid to sell out on certain features of the tradition. It should not surprise us that the dominance of Protestant liberalism coincided with the period during which this bourgeois world retained its attractiveness and, indeed, its credibility.

The First World War was the first great shock to this world – and, not surprisingly, the first serious challenge to Protestant liberalism followed it almost immediately. The disintegration of the dominance of Protestant liberalism in Europe, first on the continent and somewhat later in England, can be synchronized with the series of shocks that followed the First World War – the disintegration of the old bourgeois way of life as a taken-for-granted cultural style in the 1920s; the rise of revolutionary movements both on the left and on the right of the liberal bourgeois camp; the near-metaphysical shock of the advent of Nazism (with its first theological consequences manifested in the German *Kirchenkampf* of the 1930s); the horrors of the Second World War. In America, despite considerable differences in the character of Protestantism, there was a similar development – though with a time lag of about one generation. The First World War had not been such a great shock to the bourgeois world on this side of the Atlantic. The first great shock here came with the Great Depression, followed by the Second World War and then by the continuing crisis of the confrontation with international

Communism (the latter felt more acutely in America than in Western Europe in recent years). The first serious challenges to Protestant liberalism in America were thus not felt until the 1940s, particularly associated with the influence of Reinhold Niebuhr. We would contend that it is the difference in the infrastructural events between Europe and America that accounts for this time lag in the theological developments, rather than some alleged law of cultural diffusion between the two continents.

It goes without saying that to speak of 'dominance' in such a case does *not* mean that there was nothing else in the field. During the period in which Protestant liberalism dominated the scene there continued to exist a variety of forms of orthodoxy, with their adherents taking up stands of determined resistance to the encroachments of secular thought and pluralistic tolerance. The great reaction against liberalism, however, came after the First World War with a theological movement variously called 'dialectical' or 'neo-orthodox' and, understandably, looked upon by its liberal opponents as a postwar neurosis.[3]

The dominant figure in the movement, to this day, has been Karl Barth, and the opening shot of the assault on liberalism came in 1919, with the publication of Barth's commentary on the Letter to the Romans. Barth himself has described the effect of this publication in an apt image – that of a man climbing the steps inside a church tower in the dark, slipping and grasping for support, holding on to a rope – and then finding that, unwittingly, he has started to toll a mighty bell. What ought to be added to this image is the point that, for the ringing bell to be noticed, there must be people listening in its direction. In the German-speaking countries of central Europe, still reeling from the shattering impact of the war, Barth's mighty bell came at just the propitious moment.

Again, we cannot possibly give an account here of the development of neo-orthodox theology (to call it by the name that gained currency in America and that best describes its character). Growing steadily in the German-speaking Protestant milieu in the 1920s, the movement first encountered strong opposition, then began to gain influence rapidly in the 1930s. A good case can be made for correlating this gain with the developing struggle between Nazism and the segment of German Protestantism known as the 'Confessing Church'.[4] In this struggle Barthian neo-orthodoxy took on the character of a resistance ideology. The most important statement of the 'Confessing Church' in its effort to safeguard the Christian tradition from the *Weltanschauung* of the Nazi revolution, the so-called Barmen Declaration of 1934, was firmly based on the presuppositions of Barthian theology. Quite naturally, it also enlisted the support of some who were also opposed to Nazism but differed from Barth theologically. Generally, the Nazi situation led into the ambience of the church, particularly its 'resisting' segment (a 'resistance', it should be added, that had only a very slight *political* component), many people who under different circumstances had had no strong religious interests and certainly no inclination towards the truculently anti-modernistic theology of the Barthians. If one is to understand the rise of neo-orthodoxy in the 1930s in Europe, it is most important to remember that 'modern' at this time meant, above all, to be in accord with Nazism – in the parlance of more recent Protestantism, it was the protagonists of Nazi ideology within the church, and *not* the 'Confessing Church', who were 'relevant' to their secular situation.

Neo-orthodoxy in all its forms (to which ought to be added the revivals of orthodoxy in the Lutheran and Anglican groups) entails the energetic reassertion of the *objectivity* of the tradition (though, of course, there are differences of opinion as to just what the tradition is, say, between Barthians and neo-Lutherans). The subjectivizing, compromising, mediating efforts of liberal theology are passionately rejected – as in Barth's reply to Emil Brunner, himself clearly identified with neo-orthodoxy but more willing to make certain concessions to the 'natural' theology of liberalism, a reply appropriately entitled *Nein!* The externality and non-subjectivity of the Christian message is asserted. In Barth's own terms, God's grace is a *iustitia aliena*, coming to man from the outside and without any 'mediations' within man's own being. The Christian message is *extra nos*, sovereignly independent of the relativities of human thought and human history.

On the basis of this (in comparison with liberalism) 'Copernican revolution' in theology, neo-orthodoxy can afford to take a nonchalant attitude towards the changing fashions of secular *Weltanschauungen* and also (very importantly) towards the relativizing discoveries of historial scholarship as applied to the Christian tradition itself. Put a little crudely, the objectivity of the tradition having been defined as independent of all these contingencies, 'nothing can really happen' to the theologian. It is not difficult to see how this theological position could appear as a reliable rock on which to stand against the shifting tides of an age in turmoil. Wherever this kind of objectivity can be plausibly asserted, to this day, it serves as an 'Archimedean point' from which, in turn, all contradictory definitions of reality may be relativized.

Neo-orthodoxy has been closely associated with the so-called 'rediscovery of the Church', a new theological emphasis on the corporate character of Christianity as against liberal individualism. This linkage is anything but a mystery if one sees these developments in a sociology-of-knowledge perspective. It is not completely clear that the ecclesiastical emphasis had to follow logically from the theological presuppositions of neo-orthodoxy. One only has to recall that Kierkegaard, after all, was one of the inspirers of the movement. As the movement progressed, it dissociated itself increasingly from its 'existentialist' roots (a dissociation very marked in Barth's own theological development), to the point where today 'existentialism' is mainly a weapon in the arsenal of its opponents. We would contend that this fact makes much more sense when one reflects about the 'social engineering' imperative intrinsic to the maintenance of cognitive deviance – to wit, the imperative of constructing firm plausibility structures in the face of general social disconfirmation of the deviant definitions of reality that are to be maintained. Put crudely, if one is to believe what neo-orthodoxy wants one to believe, in the contemporary situation, then one must be rather careful to huddle together closely and continuously with one's fellow believers.

The reaffirmation of orthodox objectivities in the secularizing-pluralizing situation, then, entails the maintenance of *sectarian* forms of socio-religious organization. The sect, in its classical sociology-of-religion conception, serves as the model for organizing a cognitive minority *against* a hostile or at least non-believing milieu. This imperative manifests itself quite independently of any theological notions on the nature of the Church – it may be seen in the Catholic case (despite the universalistic, profoundly anti-sectarian character of Catholic ecclesiology), wherever Catholicism seeks to maintain itself in a massively non-Catholic milieu, and it may be seen in cases where orthodoxy or neo-orthodoxy are maintained in Protestant groups with a free-church tradition (where, of course, there exists the advantage of being able to legitimate the new sectarianism in traditional terms). The 'social engineering' imperative, however, entails a problem of promotion – to wit, people must be *motivated* to remain or to become sectarians. This is difficult in the measure that the 'outside' world is attractive. In Europe the general society became, once more, attractive a few years after the Second World War. In Germany (still the heartland of most Protestant theological movements) the turning point can be dated with embarrassing clarity in 1948 – the year of the currency reform and the beginning of economic recovery.[5] At this point, the 'outside' world, including its secularized character, becomes more difficult to see as 'the enemy', as the embodiment of 'demonic forces', and the like. Suddenly, new theological legitimations of 'secularity' make their appearance. And the dominance of neo-orthodoxy, particularly among younger theologians not of the generation of the *Kirchenkampf*, begins to decline quite rapidly.

In Germany the new theological atmosphere was established in the intensive debate over the conception of 'demythologization' developed by Rudolf Bultmann.[6] The original essay of Bultmann's proposing the 'demythologization' of the New Testament was written during the war and circulated in mimeographed form among a small group of interested theologians, but the public controversy did not erupt until its publication after the war. It dominated the German theological scene for several years and soon spread outside Germany. This time, interestingly enough, there was little if any lag between the theological developments on the two sides of the Atlantic. About the same time the Bultmann controversy emerged in Europe, Paul Tillich was beginning to publish the several volumes of his *Systematic Theology* in America.[7] Tillich's theology became a rallying point especially for younger theologians disillusioned with neo-orthodoxy, both in America and, a little later, in Europe. The new attitude towards the secular world was strongly stated by Friedrich Gogarten (who had been associated with neo-orthodoxy in the early 1920s and had broken with Barth when the latter turned away from his early existentialist leanings to a new dogmatic objectivity) in a book published in 1953.[8] It was after this that the somewhat dissonant terms 'secular theology' or 'secular Christianity' began to gain currency. The late works of Dietrich Bonhoeffer, particularly the notion of 'religionless Christianity' developed in Bonhoeffer's correspondence from prison, were widely used to legitimate the new approach, though it is far from clear whether Bonhoeffer would have gone in this direction if he had survived the war.[9] The assault on neo-orthodoxy in Germany came to a certain head in a theological manifesto put out by a group of younger theologians in 1963 and, in Barth's teeth as it were, entitled *Revelation as History*.[10]

These developments within academic theology, highly 'appropriate' to the postwar situation as we had tried to indicate, were practically begging for popularization. That prayer was answered (if the phrase may be permitted in the context of 'demythologization') by the publication of John Robinson's *Honest to God* in 1963.[11] The book immediately led to a storm of public controversy upon its publication in England – this time not in the theological journals but in the daily press and the other media of mass communication. The pattern was followed in America and in other countries where the book appeared in translation. In America the mass-media-covered controversy projected the 'new theology' into wide public awareness and was soon followed by the even more 'radical' phenomenon of the 'death of God' movement among a group of young theologians.[12] The 'new secularism' became popular not only among theologians but, significantly, among ecclesiastical organization men in search of new 'programmes'. Another best-selling book, Harvey Cox's *The Secular City*, became a sort of manifesto for this new attitude towards the secular world.[13]

Precisely because of the considerable intellectual gap between the earlier theological statements of these positions and their later 'pop' correlates it is important to see the continuity between them – a continuity lying not only on the level of the history of ideas and their popularization, but in the affinity of *both* the popularized ideas *and* their 'originals' to infrastructural developments. In this perspective, the dominance of neo-orthodoxy appears as a more or less 'accidental' interruption of the over-all process of secularization, the 'accident', of course, being the political cataclysms that brought to an end the first liberal era. The contemporary eruption of what may well be called 'neo-liberalism' thus takes up where the earlier liberalism left off, and just because of the intervening period does so in considerably more 'radical' ways. The latter fact may then also be ascribed to the more penetrating effects of secularization become more mature, as well as to the increasingly world-wide and permanent establishment of a pluralistic situation as described in the preceding chapter.

The new liberalism 'subjectivizes' religion in a radical fashion and in two senses of the word. With the progressive loss of objectivity or reality-loss of the traditional religious definitions of the world, religion becomes increasingly a matter of free subjective choice, that is, loses its intersubjectively obligatory character. Also, religious 'realities' are increasingly 'translated' from a frame of reference of facticities external to the individual consciousness to a frame of reference that locates them *within* consciousness. Thus, for example, the resurrection of Christ is no longer regarded as an event in the external world of physical nature, but is 'translated' to refer to existential or psychological phenomena in the consciousness of the believer. Put differently, the *realissimum* to which religion refers is transposed from the cosmos or from history to individual consciousness. Cosmology becomes psychology. History becomes biography. In this 'translation' process, of course, theology adapts itself to the reality presuppositions of modern secularized thought – in fact, the alleged necessity to so adapt the religious traditions (to make them 'relevant') is commonly cited as the *raison d'être* of the theological movement in question.

Various conceptual machineries have been employed in this enterprise. The concept of 'symbol', as developed in neo-Kantian philosophy, has been useful. The traditional religious affirmations can now be regarded as 'symbols' – what they supposedly 'symbolize' usually turns out to be some realities presumed to exist in the 'depths' of human consciousness. A conceptual liaison with psychologism and/or existentialism makes sense in this context and, indeed, characterizes most of contemporary neo-liberalism. Psychologism, be it of a Freudian, neo-Freudian, or Jungian variety, allows the interpretation of religion as a 'symbol system' that 'really' refers to psychological phenomena. This particular liaison has the great advantage, realized particularly in America, of legitimating religious activities as some sort of psychotherapy.[14] Since psychotherapeutic programmes are guaranteed 'instant relevance' in the American situation, this particular legitimation is very useful pragmatically from the viewpoint of religious organizations. Existentialism supplies another conceptual machinery for 'translation' purposes. If existentialist presuppositions can be posited as basic features of the human condition, religion can then be interpreted as 'symbolizing' the latter. The distinction made by German theologians between *Historie* and *Geschichte* (a distinction, alas, not possible in English) nicely illustrates the character of this 'translation' – thus the resurrection, for example, is no longer to be understood as *historisch* (that is, as an event in external, scientifically ascertainable history) but rather as *geschichtlich* (that is, as an event in the existential history of the individual). Beginning with Tillich, especially in America, both psychologistic and existentialist concepts have been employed *together* for purposes of 'translation'. Both on the level of theologically inclined intellectuals and on the level of popular 'religious interest' these concepts have shown themselves to be highly 'relevant' in the afore-mentioned sense.

Concepts derived from sociology enter the 'translation' enterprise to show that the latter is 'necessary' to begin with. As we have seen before, it is quite possible to show that modern consciousness has become highly secularized, that is, that the traditional religious affirmations have become progressively 'irrelevant' to more and more people. The neo-liberal 'translation' enterprise, however, uses sociology in a peculiar manner. It converts the sociological data from cognitive to normative statements – that is, it proceeds from the empirical constatation that certain states of consciousness in fact prevail in modern society to the epistemological assertion that these states of consciousness should serve as criteria of validity for the theologian. The theoretical possibility that the cognitive 'defect' may lie in modern consciousness rather than in the religious tradition is commonly ignored in this process.

It does not seem very likely that the extreme forms of 'radical' theology as now popularized in Protestantism will carry the field, for the simple reason that they would undermine the very existence of the religious institutions they are intended to legitimate. As legitimations they are self-defeating. The more moderate attempts, however, to bring Christianity in line with certain key reality-assumptions of secularized consciousness are most likely to continue. Specifically, the 'subjectivization' of religion, especially by means of the conceptual machinery of psychologism, may be understood as a broad trend unlikely to reverse itself in the foreseeable future – unless the course of events is once more 'interrupted' by the kind of cataclysm that brought forth neo-orthodoxy between the two world wars.

We have looked at the Protestant case in some detail, because, for reasons indicated before, it may be regarded as prototypical for the situation of religion in the modern world. The fundamental problem of legitimating a religious institution in the face of the reality-loss of its tradition is exemplified by Protestantism, which had to cope with the problem radically and early if only because it was itself an important factor in the historical genesis of that reality-loss. All other religious traditions in the orbit of Western culture, though, have had to face the same problem sooner or later. Catholicism, for reasons intrinsic to its tradition, has tried hardest in maintaining a staunchly resistant stance in the face of secularization and pluralism, and indeed has tried down to our own century to engage in vigorous counter-attacks designed to re-establish something like Christendom at least within limited territories. The fascist revolution in Spain, whose troops went into battle under banners proclaiming the kingship of Christ, was the most extreme effort in this direction. The more frequent procedure in recent times has been the retrenchment of Catholicism in subcultures within the larger society, the building of Catholic fortresses to be defended against a secular world that one could no longer hope to subject to a *reconquista*. This, of course, has raised all the 'social engineering' problems mentioned before – to wit, the 'technical' problems of keeping going a sectarian ghetto in an age of mass literacy, mass communications, and mass mobility. As long as this kind of defensiveness remained its prevalent posture, Catholicism naturally could afford little flexibility in terms of making concessions to secularized thought. In 1864 the Syllabus of Errors could still blandly condemn the notion that 'the Roman Pontiff can and ought to reconcile himself to, and agree with, progress, liberalism and civilization as lately introduced'. And the doctrine of papal infallibility was proclaimed in 1870 by Vatican I in the teeth of that 'civilization as lately introduced', which only two months later marched into Rome in the person of Victor Emmanuel. The *political* intransigence of the papacy, to be sure, was modified in the following decades, but the continuing *theological* one was well expressed in the suppression of the so-called modernist movement in the first years of the twentieth century. Particularly since Vatican II there has, of course, been a strong movement of liberalization in Catholic theology in various countries, but it may be doubted whether this will be able to go too far in modifying the profound conservatism within the institution. Indeed, if one keeps in mind the Protestant development discussed above, one must credit the conservative opponents of too radical an *aggiornamento* with a good deal of sociological instinct.

The Jewish case, again, presents quite a distinctive picture, as a result both of the peculiarities of Jewish social existence in the Western world and of Judaism as a religious tradition. Objectivity in Judaism has always been more a question of practice than of theory (more precisely, of *halachah* than of dogma), so that de-objectivation manifests itself more significantly in the disintegration of religious practice than in doctrinal heterodoxy. Also, of course, the peculiarity of Judaism as a religious tradition *and* an ethnic entity means that the problem of its plausibility *ipso facto* entails the so-called 'crisis of Jewish identity'. The Zionist attempt to redefine Jewishness in terms of a *national* identity thus has the ambivalent character of, on the one hand, re-establishing an objective plausibility structure for Jewish existence while, on the other hand, putting in question the claim of religious Judaism to being the *raison d'être* of Jewish existence – an ambivalence manifested in the ongoing difficulties between 'Church' and state in Israel. Nevertheless, the fundamental option between resistance and accommodation must be faced by Judaism, particularly in America, in terms that are not too drastically different from those in which it is faced by the Christian Churches. Specifically, the option is between defensively maintaining a Jewish subculture (which may be defined in primarily religious or primarily national terms) and playing the pluralistic game along with everyone else. It is highly indicative of this dilemma that, just when American Jewish leaders became increasingly alarmed about the threat of religious intermarriage to the continuity of the Jewish community, an important spokesman of Reform Judaism advocated that his denomination should 'evangelize' among Gentiles. In other words, even in a tradition as foreign to the spirit of pluralism as the Jewish one, the logic of the market imposes itself at the point where the 'social engineering' of subcultural defensiveness becomes too difficult.

It would take us too far afield to discuss even briefly the problems posed by secularization for non-Western religions. Suffice it to emphasize once more that modernization is today a worldwide phenomenon and that the structures of modern industrial society, despite great modifications in different areas and national cultures, produce remarkably similar situations for the religious traditions and the institutions that embody these. Indeed, because of this the experience of the Western religious traditions in modern times is of great interest if one wishes to project the future of religion in non-Western countries, regardless of whether their development takes place under socialist or non-socialist political auspices. It would be foolhardy to make detailed predictions regarding this future in any particular country. All the same, it is safe to predict that the future of religion everywhere will be decisively shaped by the forces that have been discussed in this and the preceding chapters – secularization, pluralization, and 'subjectivization' – and by the manner in which the several religious institutions will react to these.

Appendices

Appendix I

Sociological Definitions
of Religion

Definitions cannot, by their very nature, be either 'true' or 'false', only more useful or less so. For this reason it makes relatively little sense to argue over definitions. If, however, there are discrepancies between definitions in a given field, it makes sense to discuss their respective utility. This we propose to do here, with the brevity appropriate to minor matters.

Actually, a good case could be made, at least in the field of religion, that even definitions based on patently erroneous presuppositions have had a measure of utility. For example, Max Mueller's conception of religion as a 'disease of language' (*Essay on Comparative Mythology*, 1856) is based on a very inadequate rationalistic theory of language, but it is still useful in pointing to language as the great world-building instrumentality of man, reaching its most far-reaching power in the construction of the gods. Whatever else it may be, religion is a humanly constructed universe of meaning, and this construction is undertaken by linguistic means. For example, Edward Tylor's theory of animism and his conception of religion based on this theory (*Primitive Culture*, 1871) start from the quite unacceptable notion of primitive man as a sort of imperfect philosopher and, in addition, have a far too narrow emphasis on the soul as the basic religious category. Yet it is still useful to recall that religion entails man's quest for a world that will indeed be kindred to himself, that will be 'animated' in this broader sense. In sum, the only sensible attitude in matters of definition is one of relaxed tolerance.

Max Weber, at the beginning of his discussion of the sociology of religion in *Wirtschaft und Gesellschaft*, took the position that a definition of religion, if possible at all, can come only at the end, not at the beginning, of the kind of task he had set for himself. Not surprisingly, he never came to such an end, so that the reader of Weber's opus waits in vain for the promised definitional pay-off. I am not at all convinced by Weber's position on the proper sequence of definition and substantive research, since the latter can only proceed within a frame of reference that *defines* what is relevant and what is irrelevant in terms of the research. *De facto* Weber follows the definition of the scope of religion current in the *Religionswissenschaft* of his time – otherwise, for instance, he might as well have discussed the 'nation' or the *oikos* under the heading of the sociology of religion instead of the quite different headings under which they appear in *Wirtschaft und Gesellschaft*. It seems to me that the main consequence of avoiding or postponing definition in a scientific enterprise is *either* that the area of research becomes fuzzy (which most certainly is *not* the case with Weber) *or* that one operates with implicit rather than explicit definitions (which, I believe, *is* the case in Weber's work). Explication seems to me the more desirable course.

Emile Durkheim, in *The Elementary Forms of the Religious Life*, begins with a substantive description of religious phenomena, particularly in terms of the sacred/profane dichotomy, but ends with a definition in terms of the general social functionality of religion. In this, unlike Weber, he went *against* the tendency of the *religionswissenschaftliche* scholarship of the period, which tried to define religion substantively in one way or another. It may also be said, in view of this, that Durkheim's approach to religion is more radically sociological than Weber's – that is, religion is grasped as a 'social fact' in the precise Durkheimian sense.

The alternative of substantive and functional definitions is, of course, a constant in all fields of sociological analysis. Plausible arguments may be made for either choice and, indeed, one of the strongest arguments for functional definitions is that they permit a more unambiguously sociological, thus 'neater' or 'cleaner' line of analysis. I am not at all interested in taking a doctrinaire position in favour of substantive definitions at all times and in all places, but only in defending the choice of a substantive definition here.

The most convincing and far-reaching attempt to define religion in terms of its social functionality is that of Thomas Luckmann (in his *Das Problem der Religion in der modernen Gesellschaft*, 1963, English version, *The Invisible Religion*, 1967). This attempt is very clearly in the Durkheimian tradition, though it is augmented by general anthropological considerations that go considerably beyond Durkheim. Also, Luckmann is careful to differentiate between his conception of functionality and that of contemporary structural-functionalism. The functionality is grounded in certain fundamental anthropological presuppositions, *not* in particular institutional constellations that are historically relative and that cannot be validly raised to a status of universality (as, for instance, is done by sociologists of religion fixated on the Church as an institutionalization of religion peculiar to Western culture). Without going into the details of an extremely interesting argument, the essence of Luckmann's conception of religion is the capacity of the human organism to transcend its biological nature through the construction of objective, morally binding, all-embracing universes of meaning. Consequently, religion becomes not only *the* social phenomenon (as in Durkheim), but indeed *the* anthropological phenomenon *par excellence*. Specifically, religion is equated with symbolic self-transcendence. Thus everything genuinely human is *ipso facto* religious and the only non-religious phenomena in the human sphere are those that are grounded in man's animal nature, or more precisely, that part of his biological constitution that he has *in common* with other animals.

I fully share Luckmann's anthropological presuppositions (*vide* our joint theoretical effort in *The Social Construction of Reality*, 1966 – in which, logically enough, we sidestepped our difference as to the definition of religion) and I also agree with his critique of a sociology of religion fixated on the Church as a historically relative institutionalization of religion. Nevertheless,

I question the utility of a definition that equates religion with the human *tout court*. It is one thing to point up the anthropological foundations of religion in the human capacity for self-transcendence, quite another to equate the two. There are, after all, modes of self-transcendence and concomitant symbolic universes that are vastly different from each other, whatever the identity of their anthropological origins. Thus little is gained, in my opinion, by calling, say, modern science a form of religion. If one does that, one is subsequently forced to define in what way modern science is *different* from what has been called religion by everyone else, including those engaged in *Religionswissenschaft* – which poses the same definitional problem all over again. I find it much more useful to try a substantive definition of religion from the beginning, and to treat the questions of its anthropological rootage and its social functionality as separate matters.

It is for this reason that I have tried here to operate with a substantive definition of religion in terms of the positing of a *sacred cosmos* (see Chapter 1 above). The differentia in this definition, of course, is the category of the sacred, which I have taken essentially in the sense understood by *Religionswissenschaft* since Rudolf Otto (and which, incidentally, Luckmann treats as virtually interchangeable with his conception of the religious, which makes it even more difficult to differentiate between various historical forms of symbolization). This is not only the more conservative course, conceptually, but, I think, allows for less complicated distinctions between empirically available cosmoi. It must be emphasized, though, that the choice of definitions need not imply differences in the interpretation of particular socio-historical developments (as can readily be seen in those parts of the foregoing argument, particularly in chapter 6, where I not only agree with but am greatly indebted to Luckmann). In the long run, I suppose, definitions are matters of taste and thus fall under the maxim *de gustibus*.

Appendix II

Sociological and Theological Perspectives

The argument in this book has moved strictly within the frame of reference of sociological theory. No theological or, for that matter, anti-theological implications are to be sought anywhere in the argument – if anyone should believe such implications to be present *sub rosa*, I can only assure him that he is mistaken. Nor is there an intrinsic necessity for sociological theory, as here understood, to engage in a 'dialogue' with theology. The notion, still prevalent among some theologians, that the sociologist simply raises certain questions, which must then be answered by the theological partner in the 'dialogue', must be rejected on very simple methodological grounds. Questions raised within the frame of reference of an empirical discipline (and I would emphatically consider sociological theory to be within such a frame of reference) are not susceptible to answers coming out of the frame of reference of a non-empirical and normative discipline, just as the reverse procedure is inadmissible. Questions raised by sociological theory must be answered in terms falling within the latter's universe of discourse. This methodological platitude, however, does not preclude the fact that certain sociological perspectives may be *relevant* for the theologian, though in that case he will be well advised to keep the afore-mentioned discrepancy in mind when he tries to articulate that relevance within *his* universe of discourse. In sum, the argument of this book stands or falls as an enterprise of sociological theorizing and, as such, is not amenable to either theological support or theological critique.

But having said this I want, after all, to make some comments here about the relevance of this perspective to theological thinking. I have two reasons for this. First, there is the simple desire not to be misunderstood, especially not by the theologically concerned reader (for whom, let it be admitted, I have specially warm feelings). Second, I have in previous writings made statements about the relationship between sociological and theological perspectives that I no longer regard as tenable (particularly in my book *The Precarious Vision*, 1961), and I have the perhaps slightly old-fashioned notion that one ought to correct in print what one has previously said in print and no longer holds to.

Within the argument of this book itself I have felt it necessary in a few places to state that any statements made there strictly bracket the ultimate status of religious definitions of reality. I have done this particularly where I sensed the danger that the 'methodological atheism' of this type of theorizing could be misinterpreted as atheism *tout court*. I would like to stress this point again here, as strongly as I can. The essential perspective of the sociological theory here proposed is that religion is to be understood as a human projection, grounded in specific infrastructures of human history. It can be seen without much difficulty that, from the viewpoint of certain religious or ethical values, there can be both 'good' and 'bad' implications to this perspective. Thus one might feel that it is 'good' that religion protects men against anomy, but that it is 'bad' that it alienates them from the world produced by their own activity. Such valuations must be kept strictly apart from the theoretical analysis of religion as nomos and of religion as false consciousness, an analysis that, within this frame of reference, remains value-free with regard to both these aspects.

Put differently, sociological theory (and, indeed, any other theory moving within the framework of empirical disciplines) will always view religion *sub specie temporis*, thus of necessity leaving open the question whether and how it might *also* be viewed *sub specie aeternitatis*. Thus sociological theory must, by its own logic, view religion as a human projection, and by the same logic can have nothing to say about the possibility that this projection may refer to something other than the being of its projector. In other words, to say that religion is a human pro-

jection does not logically preclude the possibility that the projected meanings may have an ultimate status independent of
man. Indeed, if a religious view of the world is posited, the
anthropological ground of these projections may itself be the
reflection of a reality that *includes* both world and man, so that
man's ejaculations of meaning into the universe ultimately point
to an all-embracing meaning in which he himself is grounded. It
is not without interest to observe in this connection that it was
just such a conception that underlay Hegel's early development
of the idea of the dialectic. To be grateful, *qua* sociologist, to
Marx for his inversion of the Hegelian dialectic in the interest of
an empirical understanding of human affairs does not preclude
the possibility that, *qua* theologian, one might once more stand
Marx on *his* head – just as long as one is very clear that the two
dialectical constructions take place in strictly discrepant frames
of reference. Put simply, this would imply that man projects
ultimate meanings into reality because that reality is, indeed, ultimately meaningful, and because his own being (the empirical
ground of these projections) contains and intends these same
ultimate meanings. Such a theological procedure, if feasible,
would be an interesting ploy on Feuerbach – the reduction of
theology to anthropology would end in the reconstruction of
anthropology in a theological mode. Regretfully, I am not in a
position to offer such an intellectual man-bites-dog feat here, but
I want at least to suggest the possibility to the theologian.

The case of mathematics is rather instructive in this connection. Without any doubt mathematics is a projection on to
reality of certain structures of human consciousness. Yet the
most amazing fact about modern science is that these structures
have turned out to correspond to something 'out there' (to quote
the good Bishop Robinson). Mathematicians, physical scientists,
and philosophers of science are still trying hard to understand
just how this is possible. What is more, it is possible to show
sociologically that the development of these projections in the
history of modern thought has its origins in very specific infrastructures without which this development is most unlikely
ever to have taken place. So far nobody has suggested that *there-*

fore modern science is to be regarded as a great illusion. The parallel with the case of religion, of course, is not perfect, but it is worth reflecting on.

All this leads to the commonplace observation, frequently found in the opening pages of works in the sociology of religion, that the theologian *qua* theologian should not worry unduly over anything the sociologist may have to say about religion. At the same time, it would be foolish to maintain that *all* theological positions are equally immune to injury from the side of sociology. Logically, the theologian *will* have to worry whenever his position includes propositions that are subject to empirical disconfirmation. For example, a proposition that religion in itself is a constitutive factor of psychological well-being has a lot to worry about if subjected to sociological and social-psychological scrutiny. The logic here is similar to that of the historian's study of religion. To be sure, it can be maintained that historical and theological assertions take place in discrepant, mutually immune frames of reference. But if the theologian asserts something that can be shown to have never taken place historically or to have taken place in quite a different way from what he asserts, and if this assertion is essential to his position, then he can no longer be reassured that he has nothing to fear from the historian's work. The historical study of the Bible offers plentiful examples of this.

Sociology thus raises questions for the theologian to the extent that the latter's positions hinge on certain socio-historical pre-suppositions. For better or for worse, such presuppositions are particularly characteristic of theological thought in the Judaeo-Christian orbit, for reasons that are well known and have to do with the radically historical orientation of the Biblical tradition. The Christian theologian is, therefore, ill-advised if he simply views sociology as an ancillary discipline that will help him (or, more likely, help the practical churchman) to understand certain 'external' problems of the social environment in which his Church is located. To be sure, there are types of sociology (such as the quasi-sociological research approach that has become so popular in recent years in Church organizations) that are quite 'harmless' in this sense and can readily be appropriated for pragmatic ecclesiastical purposes. The worst that the churchman may expect from the sociologist doing religious market research for him is the unwelcome news that fewer people go to church than he thinks should go. But he will still be wise if he is careful about letting sociological analysis go too far. He may be getting more than he bargained for. Specifically, he may be getting a wider sociological perspective that may lead him on to see his over-all activity in a different light.

To repeat: on strictly methodological grounds it will be possible for the theologian to dismiss this new perspective as irrelevant to his *opus proprium*. This will become much more difficult, however, as soon as he reflects that, after all, he was not born as a theologian, that he existed as a person in a particular socio-historical situation before he ever began to do theology – in sum, that he himself, if not his theology, is illuminated by the lighting apparatus of the sociologist. At this point he may suddenly find himself ejected from the methodological sanctuary of his theologizing and find himself repeating, albeit in a very different sense, Augustine's complaint that '*Factum eram ipse mihi magna quaestio.*' He is likely to find further that, unless he can somehow neutralize this disturbing perspective in his own mind, it will be relevant to his theologizing as well. Put simply, *methodologically*, in terms of theology as a disembodied universe of discourse, sociology may be looked on as quite 'harmless' – *existentially*, in terms of the theologian as a living person with a social location and a social biography, sociology can be a very dangerous business indeed.

The *magna quaestio* of sociology is formally very similar to that of history: How, in a world of socio-historical relativity, can one arrive at an 'Archimedean point' from which to make cognitively valid statements about religious matters? In terms of sociological theory there are certain variants to this question: If all religious propositions are, at least, *also* projections grounded in specific infrastructures, how is one to distinguish between those infrastructures that give birth to truth from those that give birth to error? And if all religious plausibility is susceptible to 'social engineering', how can one be sure that those religious propositions (or, for that matter, 'religious experiences') that are plausible to oneself are not just that – products of 'social engineering' – and nothing else? It may readily be admitted that there were analogues to these questions long before sociology appeared on the scene. These may be found in the problem of Jeremiah of how to distinguish genuine and false prophecy, in the terrible doubt that apparently plagued Thomas Aquinas as to whether his own belief in the arguments for the existence of God may not after all be a matter of 'habit', in the tormenting question of numberless Christians (particularly since the Protestant schisms) of how to find the true Church. In the sociological perspective, however, such questions attain a new virulence, precisely because sociology, on its own level of analysis, gives a kind of answer to them. The vertigo of relativity that historical scholarship has brought over theological thought may thus be said to deepen in the perspective of sociology. At this point one is not much helped by the methodological assurance that theology, after all, takes place in a different frame of reference. That assurance comforts only if one is safely established in that frame of reference, if, so to speak, one already has a theology going. The existential question, however, is how one may begin to theologize in the first place.

Orthodox theological positions typically ignore this question – 'innocently' or in *mauvaise foi*, as the case may be. And indeed, for anyone who can today hold such a position 'innocently' (that is, one who has, for whatever reasons, not been touched by the vertigo of relativity) the question does not exist. Extreme theological liberalism of the variety that now calls itself 'radical theology' may be said to have despaired of finding an answer to the question and to have abandoned the attempt (*vide* the discussion of this in chapter 7). Between these two extremes there is the very interesting attempt, typical of neo-orthodoxy, to have one's cake and eat it too – that is, to absorb the full impact of the relativizing perspective, but nevertheless to posit an 'Archimedean point' in a sphere immune to relativization. This is the sphere of 'the Word', as proclaimed in the *kerygma* of the

Church and as grasped by faith. A particularly interesting point in this attempt is the differentiation between 'religion' and 'Christianity', or between 'religion' and 'faith'. 'Christianity' and 'Christian faith' are interpreted as being something quite different from 'religion'. The latter can then be cheerfully thrown to the Cerberus of relativizing analysis (historical, sociological, psychological, or what have you), while the theologian, whose concern, of course, is with 'Christianity'-which-is-not-'religion', can proceed with his work in splendid 'objectivity'. Karl Barth performed this exercise with brilliant consequence (most importantly in volume 1/2 of the *Kirchliche Dogmatik* – and with highly instructive results in his essay on Feuerbach's *Essence of Christianity*). The same procedure allowed a good many neo-orthodox theologians to come to terms with Rudolf Bultmann's 'demythologization' programme. Dietrich Bonhoeffer's fragmentary ideas on a 'religionless Christianity' were probably tending in the same direction.

It is interesting, incidentally, that a very similar possibility exists where Christianity is understood in fundamentally mystical terms. Already Meister Eckhart could distinguish between 'God' and the 'Godhead', and then go on to envisage the becoming and disbecoming of 'God'. Wherever one can maintain that, in the words of Eckhart, 'All that one can think of God, that God is not', an immune sphere is posited *ipso facto*. Relativity then touches only that which 'one can think of God' – a sphere already defined as ultimately irrelevant to the mystical truth. Simone Weil represents this possibility in recent Christian thought with great clarity.

The differentiation between 'religion' and 'Christian faith' was an important ingredient in the argument of *The Precarious Vision*, which took a neo-orthodox approach at least at that point (something, incidentally, that was perceived more clearly by some critics than by myself at the time). This differentiation, and the consequences drawn from it, now seem quite inadmissible to me. The *same* analytical tools (of historical scholarship, of sociology, and so on) can be applied to 'religion' and to 'faith'. Indeed, in any empirical discipline the 'Christian faith' is simply another case of the phenomenon 'religion'. Empirically, the differentiation makes no sense. It can only be postulated as a theological *a priori*. If one can manage this, the problem disappears. One can then deal with Feuerbach in the manner of Barth (a procedure, incidentally, that is very handy in any Christian 'dialogue' with Marxism – as long as the Marxists are agreeable to this theoretical legerdemain). But I, for one, cannot get myself into a position from which I can launch theological *a prioris*. I am forced, therefore, to abandon a differentiation that is senseless from any *a posteriori* vantage point.

If one shares this inability to hoist oneself on to an epistemologically safe platform, then no privileged status with regard to relativizing analyses can be accorded to Christianity or to any other historical manifestation of religion. The contents of Christianity, like those of any other religious tradition, will have to be analysed as human projections, and the Christian theologian will have to come to terms with the obvious discomforts caused thereby. Christianity and its various historical forms will be understood as projections similar in kind to other religious projections, grounded in specific infrastructures and maintained as subjectively real by specific processes of plausibility-generation. It seems to me that, once this is really accepted by a theologian, both the neo-orthodox and the 'radical' or neo-liberal short cut, in answer to the question as to what *else* these projections may be, are precluded. The theologian is consequently deprived of the psychologically liberating possibility of either radical commitment or radical negation. What he is left with, I think, is the necessity for a step-by-step re-evaluation of the traditional affirmations in terms of his own cognitive criteria (which need *not* necessarily be those of a putative 'modern consciousness'). Is this or that in the tradition true? Or is it false? I don't think that there are short-cut answers to such questions, neither by means of 'leaps of faith' nor by the methods of any secular discipline.

It further seems to me that such a definition of the theological situation takes one back, if not to the details, to the spirit of classical Protestant liberalism. To be sure, very few of the answers proffered by that liberalism can be replicated today in good conscience. The liberal notions of religious evolution, of the relationship between Christianity and the other world religions, of the moral dimensions of religion, and particularly of the 'ethic of Jesus' – all these can be shown to rest on untenable empirical presuppositions that very few people today would be tempted to salvage. Nor is the liberal mood of cultural optimism likely of resurrection in our own situation. The spirit of this theology, however, is more than the sum of its particular misconstructions. It is, above all, a spirit of intellectual courage that is equally removed from the cognitive retrenchment of orthodoxy and the cognitive timidity of what passes for neo-liberalism today. And it should be, one may add, a spirit that also has the courage to find itself in a cognitive minority – not only within the Church (which is hardly very painful today), but in the circles of secular intellectuals that today form the principal reference group for most theologians.

Specifically, liberal theology means to take with utmost seriousness the historicity of religion, without such theoretical subterfuges as differentiating between *Historie* and *Geschichte*, and thereby to take seriously the character of religion as a human product. This, it seems to me, must be the starting point. Only after the theologian has confronted the historical relativity of religion can he genuinely ask where in this history it may, perhaps, be possible to speak of *discoveries* – discoveries, that is, that transcend the relative character of their infrastructures. And only after he has really grasped what it means to say that religion is a human product or projection can he begin to search, *within* this array of projections, for what may turn out to be signals of transcendence. I strongly suspect that such an inquiry will turn increasingly from the projections to the projector, that is, will become an enterprise in anthropology. An 'empirical theology' is, of course, methodologically impossible. But a theology that proceeds in a step-by-step correlation with what can be said about man empirically is well worth a serious try.

It is in such an enterprise that a conversation between sociology and theology is most likely to bear intellectual fruits. It will be clear from the above that this will require partners, on both sides, with a high degree of openness. In the absence of such partners, silence is by far the better course.

Notes

Chapter 1

1. The term 'world' is here understood in a phenomenological sense, that is, with the question of its ultimate ontological status remaining in brackets. For the anthropological application of the term, cf. Max Scheler, *Die Stellung des Menschen im Kosmos* (Munich, Nymphenburger Verlagshandlung, 1947). For the application of the term to the sociology of knowledge, cf. Max Scheler, *Die Wissensformen und die Gesellschaft* (Bern, Francke, 1960); Alfred Schutz, *Der sinnhafte Aufbau der sozialen Welt* (Vienna, Springer, 1960), and *Collected Papers,* Vols. I–II (The Hague, Nijhoff, 1962–4). The term 'dialectic' as applied to society is here understood in an essentially Marxian sense, particularly as the latter was developed in the *Economic and Philosophical Manuscripts of 1844.*

2. We would contend that this dialectic understanding of man and society as mutual products makes possible a theoretical synthesis of the Weberian and Durkheimian approaches to sociology without losing the fundamental intention of either (such a loss having occurred, in our opinion, in the Parsonian synthesis). Weber's understanding of social reality as ongoingly constituted by human signification and Durkheim's of the same as having the character of *choseité* as against the individual are *both* correct. They intend respectively, the subjective foundation and the objective facticity of the societal phenomenon, *ipso facto* pointing towards the dialectic relationship of subjectivity and its objects. By the same token, the two understandings are only correct *together.* A quasi-Weberian emphasis on subjectivity *only* leads to an idealistic distortion of the societal phenomenon. A quasi-Durkheimian emphasis on objectivity *only* leads to sociological reification, the more disastrous distortion towards which much of contemporary Am-

erican sociology has tended. It should be stressed that we are not implying here that such a dialectic synthesis would have been agreeable to these two authors themselves. Our interest is systematic rather than exegetical, an interest that permits an eclectic attitude towards previous theoretical constructions. When we say, then, that the latter 'intend' such a synthesis, we mean this in the sense of intrinsic theoretical logic rather than of the historical intentions of these authors.

3. The terms 'externalization' and 'objectivation' are derived from Hegel (*Entaeusserung* and *Versachlichung*), and understood here essentially as they were applied to collective phenomena by Marx. The term 'internalization' is understood as commonly used in American social psychology. The theoretical foundation of the latter is above all the work of George Herbert Mead, for which cf. his *Mind, Self and Society* (Chicago, University of Chicago Press, 1934); Anselm Strauss (ed.), *George Herbert Mead on Social Psychology* (Chicago, University of Chicago Press, 1956); *Social Psychology* (Chicago, London 1964 – Phoenix Books no. P170). The term 'reality *sui generis*', as applied to society, is developed by Durkheim in his *Rules of Sociological Method* (Glencoe, Ill., Free Press, 1950; London, Collier-Macmillan, 1964).

4. The anthropological necessity of externalization was developed by Hegel and Marx. For more contemporary developments of this understanding, in addition to the work of Scheler, cf. Helmut Plessner, *Die Stufen des Organischen und der Mensch* (1928), and Arnold Gehlen, *Der Mensch* (1940).

5. For the biological foundation of this argument, cf. F. J. J. Buytendijk, *Mensch und Tier* (Hamburg, Rowohlt, 1958); Adolf Portmann, *Zoologie und des neue Bild des Menschen* (Hamburg, Rowohlt, 1956). The most important application of these biological perspectives to sociological problems is to be found in the work of Gehlen.

6. This has been succinctly put in the opening sentence of a recent anthropological work written from an essentially Marxian viewpoint: 'L'homme naît inachevé' (Georges Lapassade, *L'entrée dans la vie* [Paris, Editions de Minuit, 1963], p. 17).

7. Plessner has coined the term 'eccentricity' to refer to this innate instability in man's relationship to his own body. cf. op. cit.

8. The use of the term 'culture' to refer to the totality of man's products follows the current practice in American cultural

anthropology. Sociologists have tended to use the term in a narrower sense as referring only to the so-called symbolic sphere (thus Parsons in his concept of the 'cultural system'). While there are good reasons to prefer the narrower sense in other theoretical contexts, we have felt that the broader use is more appropriate in the present argument.

9. The linkage of material and non-material production was developed in Marx's concept of 'labour' (which cannot be understood as merely an economic category).

10. There are, of course, different concepts of society in use among sociologists. A discussion of these would serve little purpose in this argument. We have, therefore, used a very simple definition, relating it to the afore-mentioned concept of culture.

11. The understanding of 'human nature' as itself a human product is also derived from Marx. It marks the fundamental split between a dialectic and a non-dialectic anthropology. Within sociological thought, these anthropological antipodes are best represented, respectively, by Marx and Pareto. The Freudian anthropology, incidentally, must also be designated as an essentially non-dialectic one, a point commonly overlooked in recent attempts at a Freudian-Marxian synthesis.

12. The essential sociality of man was clearly seen by Marx, but it is, of course, endemic to the entire sociological tradition. The work of Mead provides an indispensable social-psychological basis for Marx's anthropological insights.

13. The necessity for sociology to dehypostatize the social objectivations was repeatedly stressed in Weber's methodology. Although it is probably wrong to accuse Durkheim of a hypostatized conception of society (as a number of Marxist critics have done), his method easily lends itself to this distortion, as has been shown particularly in its development by the structural-functionalist school.

14. For a development of the understanding of shared objectivity, cf. the previously cited works of Schutz.

15. The discussion of the objectivity of society closely follows Durkheim at this point. cf. especially the previously cited *Rules of Sociological Method*.

16. The understanding of language as paradigmatic for the objectivity of social phenomena is also derived from Durkheim. For a discussion of language in essentially Durkheimian terms, cf. A. Meillet, *Linguistique historie et linguistique générale* (Paris, Champion, 1958).

17. For the reality of self-interpretations as location in an objectively real social world, cf. the work of Maurice Halbwachs on memory, especially his *Les Cadres sociaux de la mémoire* (Paris, Presses Universitaires de France, 1925).

18. The concept of roles as objective representation is arrived at by a combination of Meadian and Durkheimian viewpoints. On the latter, cf. here especially Durkheim's *Sociology and Philosophy* (London, Cohen & West, 1953), pp. 1ff.

19. The concept of internal conversation is derived from Mead. cf. his *Mind, Self and Society*, pp. 135ff.

20. The term 'significant others' is also derived from Mead. It has, of course, gained general currency in American social psychology.

21. We would contend that this affirmation of introspection as a viable method for the understanding of social reality *after* successful socialization may serve to bridge the apparently contradictory propositions of Durkheim about the subjective opaqueness of social phenomena and of Weber about the possibility of *Verstehen*.

22. The dialectical character of socialization is expressed in Mead's concepts of the 'I' and the 'me'. cf. op. cit., pp. 173ff.

23. The term 'nomos' is indirectly derived from Durkheim by, as it were, turning around his concept of *anomie*. The latter was first developed in his *Suicide* (Glencoe, Ill., Free Press, 1951); cf. especially pp. 241ff. (London, Routledge & Kegan Paul, 1952).

24. The definition of social action in terms of meaning derives from Weber. The implications of this definition in terms of the social 'world' were especially developed by Schutz.

25. The term 'totalization' is derived from Jean-Paul Sartre. cf. his *Critique de la raison dialectique*, Vol. 1 (Paris, Gallimard, 1960); *The Problem of Method*, trans. Hazel E. Barnes (London, Methuen, 1963).

26. 'Anomy' is an Anglicization of Durkheim's *anomie* favoured by several American sociologists, though not by Robert Merton (who sought to integrate the concept within his structural-functionalist theory, retaining the French spelling). We have adopted the Anglicized spelling for stylistic reasons only.

27. This suggests that there are nomic as well as anomic suicides, a point alluded to but not developed by Durkheim in his discussion of 'altruistic suicide' (*Suicide*, pp. 217ff.).

28. The concept of 'marginal situations' (*Grenzsituationen*) derives from Karl Jaspers. cf. especially his *Philosophie* (1932).

29. The notion of the 'other aspect' of reality has been developed by Robert Musil in his great unfinished novel, *Der Mann ohne Eigenschaften*, in which it is a major theme. *The Man Without Qualities*, trans. Eithne Wilkins and Ernst Kaiser (London, Secker & Warburg, 1953). For a critical discussion, cf. Ernst Kaiser and Eithne Wilkins, *Robert Musil* (Stuttgart, Kollhammer, 1962).

30. The concept of death as the most important marginal situation is derived from Martin Heidegger. cf. especially his *Sein und Zeit* (1929); *Being and Time*, trans. John Macquarrie and Edward Robinson (London, S.C.N. Press, 1962).

31. The concept of the world-taken-for-granted is derived from Schutz. cf. especially his *Collected Papers*, Vol. 1, pp. 207ff.

32. The term 'cosmization' is derived from Mircea Eliade. cf. his *Cosmos and History* (New York, Harper, 1959), pp. 10ff.; *Myth and Reality* (London, Allen & Unwin, 1964).

33. The concept of projection was first developed by Ludwig Feuerbach. Both Marx and Nietzsche derived it from the latter. It was the Nietzschean derivation that became important for Freud.

34. This definition is derived from Rudolf Otto and Mircea Eliade. For a discussion of the problem of defining religion in a sociological context, cf. Appendix I. Religion is defined here as a human enterprise because this is how it manifests itself as an empirical phenomenon. Within this definition the question as to whether religion may also be something more than that remains bracketed, as, of course, it must be in any attempt at scientific understanding.

35. For a clarification of the concept of the sacred, cf. Rudolf Otto, *Das Heilige* (Munich, Beck, 1963); *The Idea of the Holy*, trans. John W. Harvey (Penguin Books, Harmondsworth, 1959), Pelican Books No. A452; Gerardus van der Leeuw, *Religion in Essence and Manifestation* (London, George Allen & Unwin, 1938); Mircea Eliade, *Das Heilige und das Profane* (Hamburg, Rowohlt, 1957); *The Sacred and the Profane*, trans. William R. Tresk (New York, Harper & Row, 1961). The dichotomy of the sacred and the profane is used by Durkheim in his *The Elementary Forms of the Religious Life*, trans. J. W. Swain (New York, Collier Books, 1961; London, Allen & Unwin, 1915).

36. cf. Eliade, *Cosmos and History, passim*.

37. cf. Eliade, *Das Heilige und das Profane*, p. 38. 'Die Welt laesst

sich als "Welt", als "Kosmos" insofern fassen, als sie sich als heilige Welt offenbart.'

Chapter 2

1. The term 'legitimation' is derived from Weber, although it is used here in a broader sense.

2. The concentration on theoretical ideation has been one of the major weaknesses of the sociology of knowledge as generally understood so far. The work of the present writer in the sociology of knowledge has been greatly influenced by the insistence of Schutz that the sociologically most relevant knowledge is precisely that of the man in the street, that is, 'commonsense knowledge', rather than the theoretical constructions of intellectuals.

3. On the microcosm/macrocosm scheme, cf. Mircea Eliade, *Cosmos and History* (New York, Harper, 1959), and Eric Voegelin, *Order and History*, Vol. I (Baton Rouge, Louisiana State University Press, 1956). Voegelin's conception of 'cosmological civilizations' and their rupture through what he calls 'leaps in being' is of great importance for the present argument.

4. On the 'cosmic' implications of kinship structure, cf. Durkheim's *Elementary Forms of the Religious Life* (New York, Collier Books, 1961; London, Allen & Unwin, 1915). Also, cf. Claude Lévi-Strauss, *Les structures élémentaires de la parenté* (Paris, Presses Universitaires de France, 1949), and *La Pensée sauvage* (Paris, Plon, 1962).

5. On transformations of the microcosm/macrocosm scheme, cf. Voegelin, op. cit., especially the introductory chapter.

6. On the sociological implications of the microcosm/macrocosm scheme, cf. Weber's works on the sociology of the religions of India and China. Also, cf. Marcel Granet, *La Pensée chinoise* (Paris, Albin Michel, 1934).

7. For a detailed analysis of the break through the microcosm/macrocosm scheme in Israel and in Greece, cf. Voegelin, op. cit., Vol. I and Vols. II–III, respectively.

8. On religious legitimation in Israel, cf. R. de Vaux, *Les institutions de l'Ancien Testament* (Paris, Editions du Cerf, 1961); *Studies in Old Testament Sacrifice* (University of Wales Press, Cardiff, 1964). This important work is now available in an English translation.

9. On religious legitimation in Greece and Rome, the classic work

for the sociology of religion is still Fustel de Coulanges's *The Ancient City*, trans. W. Small (London, Simpkin Marshall, 1916). This work is particularly interesting because of its influence on Durkheim's thinking about religion.

10. On divine kingship, cf. Henri Frankfort, *Kingship and the Gods* (Chicago, University of Chicago Press, 1948).

11. This discussion of course, applies some important concepts of George Herbert Mead to the social psychology of religion.

12. This discussion of roles as 'representations' is indebted both to Durkheim and to Mead, with the Durkheimian term being placed in the context of a Meadian approach to social psychology.

13. ' "How does one create a memory for the human animal? How does one go about to impress anything on that partly dull, partly flighty human intelligence – that incarnation of forgetfulness – so as to make it stick?" As we might well imagine, the means used in solving this age-old problem have been far from delicate: in fact, there is perhaps nothing more terrible in man's earliest history than his mnemotechnics. "A thing is branded on the memory to make it stay there; only what goes on hurting will stick" – this is one of the oldest and, unfortunately, one of the most enduring psychological axioms . . . Whenever man has thought it necessary to create a memory for himself, his effort has been attended with torture, blood, sacrifice.' *Vide* Friedrich Nietzsche, *The Genealogy of Morals* (Garden City, N.Y., Doubleday-Anchor, 1956), pp. 192f.; Friedrich Nietzsche, *Complete Works*, Vol. 13 (London and Edinburgh, T. N. Foulis, 1910).

14. The conception of religion as embedded in ritual was strongly emphasized by Durkheim, who influenced Robert Will in the latter's important work *Le Culte*. Also, cf. S. Mowinckel, *Religion und Kultur* (1953), and H. J. Kraus, *Gottesdienst in Israel* (1954).

15. The sharpest formulation of this point in sociological literature is by Maurice Halbwachs: 'La pensée sociale est essentiellement une mémoire.' *Vide* Halbwachs, *Les cadres sociaux de la mémoire* (Paris, Presses Universitaires de France, 1952), p. 296.

16. This discussion is strongly indebted to the Marxian conception of the dialectical relationship between sub- and superstructure (*Unterbau* and *Ueberbau*), the former to be identified *not* with an economic '*base*' but with *praxis* in general. How far this conception is in logical contradiction with Weber's understanding of the

'elective affinity' (*Wahlverwandtschaft*) between certain religious ideas and their social 'carriers' (*Traeger*) is an interesting question. Weber, of course, thought so. But we would contend that this conviction of his is not unrelated to the fact that his work antedated by more than a decade the reinterpretation of Marx stimulated by the rediscovery, in 1932, of the *Economic and Philosophical Manuscripts of 1844*. For a very interesting discussion of religion (specifically, religion in seventeenth-century France) in terms of a Marxian sociology of religion, cf. Lucien Goldmann, *Le Dieu caché* (Paris, Gallimard, 1956).

17. The term 'marginal situation' is derived from Jaspers, but its use in this discussion is strongly influenced by Schutz, particularly by the latter's analysis of the relationship between the 'paramount reality' of everyday life and what he called 'finite provinces of meaning'. cf. Schutz, *Collected Papers,* Vol. 1 (The Hague, Nijhoff, 1962), pp. 207ff.

18. Even today, of course, religion has to cope with such 'marginal' realities. The current efforts to integrate religion with the 'findings' of 'depth psychology' may serve as an important illustration. These efforts, it may be added, presuppose that the reality-definitions of the psychologists have become more plausible than the ones of traditional religion.

19. The conception of death as the most important marginal situation is derived from Heidegger, but Schutz's analysis of the 'fundamental anxiety' developed this within his over-all theory of the reality of everyday life.

20. The concept of plausibility structure, as defined here, incorporates some key understandings of Marx, Mead, and Schutz.

21. For an excellent discussion of this, cf. Gustave von Grunebaum, *Medieval Islam* (Chicago, University of Chicago Press, 1961), pp. 31ff.

22. One of the important weaknesses of Durkheim's sociological theory of religion is the difficulty of interpreting within its framework religious phenomena that are *not* society-wide – in the terms used here, the difficulty of dealing in Durkheimian terms with subsocietal plausibility structures. Weber's analysis of the differences between the 'Church' and 'sect' types of religious sociation is very suggestive in this connection, although Weber did not develop the *cognitive* (in a sociology-of-knowledge sense) implications of sectarianism. For the social psychology of reality-maintenance, cf. Leon Festinger, *A Theory of Cognitive Dis-*

sonance (Evanston, Ill., Row, Peterson & Co., 1957; London, Tavistock Publications, 1962); Milton Rokeach, *The Open and the Closed Mind* (New York, Basic Books, 1960); and Hans Toch, *The Social Psychology of Social Movements* (Indianapolis, Bobbs-Merrill, 1965).

23. The classic psychological account of conversion remains the one in William James's *Varieties of Religious Experience* (London, Longmans, 1902 and many editions), but much light on its social prerequisites has been shed by recent studies of the cognitive bargaining' going on in 'group dynamics' and in psychotherapy, as well as in coercive political indoctrination of the 'brainwashing' type.

Chapter 3

1. This definition is, of course, broader than the usage of the term in Christian theological thought, where it has its origin. In this we follow Weber, as indeed this entire chapter leans heavily on the latter's discussion of theodicy. cf. especially the section on 'Das Problem der Theodizee', in *Wirtschaft und Gesellschaft* (Tuebingen, Mohr, 1947), Vol. I, pp. 296ff. For an English translation, cf. *The Sociology of Religion,* trans. Ephraim Fischoff (Boston, Beacon, 1963), pp. 138ff.; (London, Methuen, 1965).

2. Weber distinguishes between four rational types of theodicy – the promise of compensation in this world; the promise of compensation in a 'beyond'; dualism; the doctrine of *karma*. Our discussion here is based on this typology, though some modifications are introduced.

3. The notion of the self-transcending character of religion was developed by Durkheim, especially in his *Elementary Forms of the Religious Life*, trans. J. W. Swain (New York, Collier Books, 1961; London, Allen & Unwin, 1915). We have tried here to draw the implications of this Durkheimian insight for the problem of theodicy.

4. The concept of masochism employed here is derived from Sartre, as he developed it in his *Being and Nothingness*, trans. Hazel E. Barnes (London, Methuen, 1957). It is emphatically *not* to be understood in Freudian or other psychoanalytic terms. The Sartrian concept of masochism may also be understood as a particular mode of self-reification (understanding the term 'reification' in a

Marxian sense). For the psychiatric implications of the Marxian concept, cf. Joseph Gabel, *La fausse conscience* (Paris, Editions de Minuit, 1962).

5. Sartre developed in considerable detail the predestined failure of the masochistic enterprise.

6. The notion of the possible meaning of 'becoming nothingness' is derived from Nietzsche. We would leave open the question whether this phenomenon could in any way be related to Freud's 'death instinct'.

7. We would contend that this perspective provides a useful starting point for a critique of Freudian libido theory. A critique along these lines can be found in so-called 'Phenomenological psycho-analysis', as in the works of Binswanger, Minkowski, Frankl, and others.

8. It is important to understand that theodicy is possible without any promise of 'redemption'. In other words, soteriology is not co-extensive with religion. This point is strongly made by Weber in the sociology-of-religion section of *Wirtschaft und Gesellschaft*.

9. This point was also made by Weber, in his understanding of 'double theodicy'. In this, he incorporates and at the same time goes beyond Marx's conception of religion as an 'opiate'.

10. Our understanding is, again, derived from Weber.

11. The Weberian typology is modified here by placing its types within a rational-irrational continuum.

12. Lévy-Bruhl's concept of 'mystic participation' is applicable here.

13. This point, of course, is strongly made in Durkheim's theory of *anomie*, particularly in his *Suicide* (London, Collier-Macmillan, 1966).

14. In addition to Durkheim's *Elementary Forms of the Religious Life*, trans. J. W. Swain (London, Allen & Unwin, second impression 1928), cf. Bronislaw Malinowski, *Magic, Science and Religion* (Garden City, N.Y., Doubleday-Anchor, 1954).

15. cf. Mircea Eliade, *Das Heilige und das Profane* (Hamburg, Rowohlt, 1957), pp. 68ff.

16. cf. Johannes Pedersen, *Israel* (Copenhagen, Branner og Korch, 1926), pp. 253ff., for an analysis of this phenomenon in the ancient Near East. Trans. M. A. Hollen (London, Humphrey Milford, 1926).

17. cf. Mircea Eliade, *Cosmos and History* (New York, Harper, 1959), pp. 93ff.

18. cf. Gerardus van der Leeuw, *Religion in Essence and Manifestation* (London, George Allen & Unwin, 1938), pp. 493ff. One of the most penetrating analyses of the cross-cultural similarity of mysticism may be found in Rudolf Otto's *Mysticism East and West*; trans. Bertha L. Bracey and Richenda C. Payne (London, Macmillan, 1932).

19. Reynold Nicholson (ed.), *Rumi — Poet and Mystic* (London, George Allen & Unwin, 1950), p. 103. The italicized phrases are quotations of, respectively, Quran 28: 88 and 2: 151. It may be left open here whether Rumi intends this passage to refer to actual reincarnations or to stations on a mystical journey.

20. Weber thus characterized the *karma-samsara* doctrine. For general discussions, cf. S. Chatterjee. *The Fundamentals of Hinduism* (Calcutta, Das Gupta, 1950); Louis Renou, *L'hindouisme* (Paris, Albin Michel, 1951), and *Religions of Ancient India* (New York, Oxford University Press, 1953). The classical sociological discussion, of course, is to be found in the second volume of Weber's *Gesammelte Aufsaetze zur Religionssoziologie.*

21. 'Die Welt ist ein lueckenloser Kosmos ethischer Vergeltung.' Weber, *Wirtschaft und Gesellschaft*, Vol. I, p. 300.

22. This point was analysed in detail by Weber.

23. Sarvepalli Radhakrishnan and Charles Moore (eds.), *A Source Book in Indian Philosophy* (Princeton, Princeton University Press, 1957), p. 93.

24. *Vide* Weber's analysis of the soteriologies of Indian 'intellectuals' and their relationship to the Hinduism of the masses.

25. Radhakrishnan and Moore, loc. cit.

26. It is evident that these remarks are, in a sense, a 'terrible simplification' of what is historically an immensely complicated and variegated agglomeration of soteriological ideas. They are justified to the extent that they indicate the basic alternatives open to theodicies constructed on the presupposition of *karma-samsara*. Similar protestations of modesty, of course, ought properly to be made with respect to the other historical typifications of this chapter.

27. Weber regarded Buddhism as the most radical rationalization of the *karma-samsara* complex. In addition to Weber's discussion of Buddhism, both in *Wirtschaft und Gesellschaft* and in the *Gesammelte Aufsaetze zur Religionssoziologie*, cf. the discussion of the Buddhist conception of *karma* (*kamma* in the Pali canonical writings) in C. A. F. Rhys Davids, *Buddhism* (London,

S.P.C.K., 1912), and *A Manual of Buddhism* (London, S.P.C.K., 1932); Richard Gard, *Buddhism* (New York, Braziller, 1961; London, Prentice Hall International 1961).

28. We are, again, closely following Weber here, except that the term 'intermediate', of course, does not occur in his analysis and is introduced here to develop the concept of a rational-irrational continuum of theodicies.

29. cf. W. E. Muehlmann (ed.), *Chiliasmus und Nativismus* (Berlin, 1961); Sylvia Thrupp (ed.), *Millennial Dreams in Action* (The Hague, 1962).

30. The work of Leon Festinger on the psychology of 'cognitive dissonance' is very relevant here – *vide* both his *Theory of Cognitive Dissonance* (London, Tavistock Publications, 1962) and the earlier case study, *When Prophecy Fails* (New York, Harper & Row, 1964). The similarity of the phenomena analysed in the case study with what New Testament scholars have called *Parousieverzoegerung* is astonishing and highly instructive.

31. cf. Van der Leeuw, op. cit., pp. 275ff. Also cf. E. Rohde, *Psyche*, trans. W. B. Hillis (London, Kegan Paul, 1925), and William Greene, *Moira* (Cambridge, Mass., Harvard University Press, 1944), for the problem of theodicy in Greek religious thought.

32. On the development of Israelite theodicy, cf. Gerhard von Rad's *Theologie des alten Testaments,* particularly Vol. II, and Edmond Jacob, *Théologie de l'Ancien Testament* (Neuchâtel, Delachaux & Niestlé, 1955), pp. 240ff.; *Theology of the Old Testament,* trans. Arthur W. Heathcote and Philip J. Allcock (London, Hodder & Stoughton, 1958). On the highly suggestive episode of Shabbatai Zvi, cf. Gershom Scholem, *Major Trends in Jewish Mysticism* (New York, Schocken, 1961), pp. 287ff.; (London, Thames & Hudson, 1955).

33. cf. W. Hinz, *Zarathustra* (Stuttgart, 1961); Franz Altheim, *Zarathustra und Alexander* (Frankfurt, 1960); Maarten Vermaseren, *Mithras* (Stuttgart, 1965); *Mithras the Secret God,* trans. Thérèse and Vincent Megaw (London, Chatto & Windus, 1963); R. Reitzenstein, *Das iranische Erloesungsmysterium* (Bonn, 1921).

34. cf. Hans Jonas, *The Gnostic Religion* (Boston, Beacon, 1963). The classic work on Marcion is Adolf von Harnack's *Das Evangelium vom fremden Gott.* On the Albigensians, cf. S. Runciman, *The Medieval Manichee* (Cambridge, 1947).

35. Jonas, op, cit., p. 54.

36. cf. Scholem, op. cit., pp. 40ff.; Adolf von Harnack, *Dogmengeschichte* (Tuebingen, Mohr, 1922), pp. 63ff.; *Outlines of the History of Dogma* (Boston, Starr King Press, and London, Ernest Benn, 1960); Reynold Nicholson, *The Mystics of Islam* (London, Bell, 1914).

37. In this discussion of the development of the Biblical theodicy we depart completely from Weber. It is indeed very curious that Weber's interest in the Christian theodicy was pretty much limited to its 'radicalized' outcome in the Calvinist doctrine of predestination – a curious fact, despite its obvious relationship to Weber's concern with the historical role of Calvinism.

38. Weber explicitly drew the comparison between Islam and Calvinism in terms of predestination.

39. The term 'religious virtuosi' is taken from Weber.

40. The modification of the original 'starkness' of Calvinism is, of course, one of the major themes of Weber's argument in *The Protestant Ethic and the Spirit of Capitalism*.

41. Weber appears to have been quite oblivious of the essential place of Christology in any Christian theodicy – part of the curious fact already remarked upon above. We would contend that this is a major weakness of his general typology of theodicies.

42. Albert Camus, *The Rebel*, trans. Anthony Bowen (New York, Vintage, 1953), p. 34; (London, Hamish Hamilton, 1953).

43. 'Ist das Goettliche, das auf Erden erschienen ist und die Menschen mit Gott wiedervereinigt hat, identisch mit dem hoechsten Goettlichen, das Himmel und Erde regiert, oder ist es ein Halbgoettliches? Das war die entscheidende Frage im arianischen Streit.' Harnack, *Dogmengeschichte*, p. 210.

44. We omit here any discussion of the different theological answers to the question as to the precise relationship of Christ's suffering to the accomplishment of redemption. cf. Gustaf Aulén, *Christus Victor* (London, S.P.C.K., 1931), for a useful typology. Also cf. John Hick, *Evil and the God of Love* (New York, Harper & Row, and London, Macmillan, 1966).

45. The analyses of Christianity by Marx and Nietzsche are, of course, the most important cases of this.

46. Camus, op. cit., p. 56.

47. Recent controversies among Marxists about the relationship of other over-all *Weltanschauung* to the concrete problems of meaning in individual life are a good illustration of this. cf. Erich

Fromm (ed.), *Socialist Humanism* (Garden City, N.Y., Doubleday, 1965).

Chapter 4

1. The concept of the duplication of consciousness is derived from Mead. Durkheim's notion of socialized man as *homo duplex* is also relevant.

2. This formulation seeks to combine key Marxian and Meadian perspectives.

3. The term 'social self' was used by William James. Its development, through the work of James Baldwin and Charles Cooley to its, as it were, 'codification' by Mead, is of decisive importance for American social psychology.

4. The concept of internal conversation is derived from Mead.

5. The concept of alienation used here is, of course, derived from Marx, though we have modified the sharpness with which Marx set off his use of the concept against Hegel's. Particularly, we have not followed Marx in his pseudo-theological notion that alienation is the result of certain historical 'sins' of the social order or in his utopian hopes for the abolition of alienation (that is, its *Aufhebung*) through the socialist revolution. We would, therefore, readily agree that our use of the concept has 'right' rather than 'left' implications. For one of the most helpful discussions of the concept from a non-Marxist viewpoint, cf. the essay 'Ueber die Geburt der Freiheit aus der Entfremdung' by Arnold Gehlen, in his *Studien zur Anthropologie und Soziologie* (Neuwied/Rhein, Luchterhand, 1963), pp. 232ff. For an earlier treatment of the matter by the author, cf. Peter Berger and Stanley Pullberg, 'Reification and the Sociological Critique of Consciousness', *History and Theory*, IV: 2 (1965), 196ff.

6. The formulation is a paraphrase of Vico's classic statement on the difference between history and nature.

7. The concept of false consciousness is used here in an essentially Marxian sense, though with the shift of meaning already indicated with regard to alienation.

8. On the history of the concept of reification, cf. Berger and Pullberg, loc. cit.

9. cf. ibid., p. 204, footnote 13. To say that alienation is a phenomenon of consciousness is not to deny that it is originally prereflective, nor that it is grounded in *praxis*. It is rather to avoid

the misleading conclusion that alienated man no longer is a world-producing being.

10. This once more separates us from what we would consider Marx's utopian perspective. We accept the distinction made by Marx, against Hegel, between objectivation (*Versachlichung*)/externalization (*Entaeusserung*) and reification (*Verdinglichung*)/alienation (*Entfremdung*), as well as Marx's notion that the latter two processes, unlike the first two, are not to be understood as anthropological necessities. However, we cannot go along with Marx's notion (further vulgarized later on by Engels) that alienation *historically succeeds* a state of non-alienated being.

11. The work of Lévy-Bruhl on 'primitive mentality' and that of Piaget on the thinking of children is highly relevant here. For recent treatments of these matters, cf. Claude Lévi-Strauss, *La pensée sauvage* (Paris, Plon, 1962); Jean Piaget, *Etudes sociologiques* (Geneva, Droz, 1965), pp. 143ff.

12. cf. Berger and Pullberg, loc. cit., pp. 209f.

13. The theoretical confusion between alienation and anomy is central to almost everything that has recently been written by American social scientists on these concepts. The confusion is further aggravated by the psychologization of both concepts.

14. The basic association between religion and alienation was made by Feuerbach. Not only Marx but also Nietzsche and Freud were influenced by Feuerbach in their conception of religion.

15. cf. Rudolf Otto, *Das Heilige* (Munich, Beck, 1963), pp. 28ff.; *The Idea of the Holy*, trans. John W. Harvey (Penguin, Harmondsworth, 1959: Pelican A452).

16. Swami Nikhilananda (trans.), *The Bhagavad Gita* (New York, Ramakrishna-Vivekananda Center, 1944), pp. 126f.

17. ibid., p. 130.

18. Otto strongly insisted on the continuing element of 'otherness' even in more sophisticated forms of religion.

19. In Schutzian terms, they are available only as 'finite provinces of meaning', surrounded by the 'paramount reality' of the everyday life shared with other men. *Vide* Appendix II for a brief discussion of the possible theological implications of this.

20. The term 'projection' was first used in this sense by Feuerbach. cf. the following early formulation in Feuerbach's essay 'Zur Kritik der positiven Philosophie' (*Hallische Jahrbuecher*, 1838): 'Die absolute Persoenlichkeit – das ist Gott als die *Projektion des eigenen Wesens*: eine *Illusion*, dass das Object seiner Spekulation

nicht sein eigenes Selbst, sondern ein anderes, das goettliche ist!' The concept of projection expresses the central perspective of Feuerbach's lifelong interest in religion, which reached its clearest expression in his *Das Wesen des Christentums* (1841); *The Essence of Christianity*, trans. Marian Evans (London, J. Chapman, 1953). Marx's major modification of the perspective was the insistence that the religious projection is a *collective* one. It should be noted, though, that Marx does not use the term 'projection', despite its ready applicability to his own thought.

21. It should be emphasized that, in refusing to *equate* religion and alienation, we are again deviating from the Marxian conception as well as from Feuerbach's.

22. The term 'mystification' is derived from Marx.

23. The term 'bad faith' (*mauvaise foi*) is derived from Sartre.

24. A Meadian formulation of this might be: The 'me' is apprehended as totally incorporating the 'I'.

25. The term 'total dependence' was used by Schleiermacher in his analysis of religious 'experience'.

26. The term 'reflection', in this sense, has been used by Lenin and is typical of so-called 'vulgar Marxism'. Our proposition, by contrast, again applies to religion what we would consider to be the original Marxian understanding of the *dialectical* relationship between sub- and superstructure.

27. This one-sidedness, of course, is the principal weakness of Marx's own and the later Marxist approach to religion.

28. Sarvepalli Radhakrishnan and Charles Moore (eds.), *A Source Book in Indian Philosophy* (Princeton, Princeton University Press, 1957), p. 91.

29. Weber's principal focus in his analysis of Indian soteriologies was, of course, on their different implications for everyday social and economic conduct. For an elaborate survey of Hindu ethical systems, cf. P. V. Kane, *History of Dharmasastra* (Poona, Bhandarkar Oriental Research Institute, 1930–62). On the theoretical development of the concept of *maya* in Vedanta thought, cf. Paul Deussen, *Das System der Vedanta* (Leipzig, Brockhaus, 1921); *Outline of the Vedanta System of Philosophy* (Cambridge, Mass., Harvard University Press, and London, Oxford University Press, 1915); also, A. K. R. Chandhuri, *The Doctrine of Maya* (Calcutta, Das Gupta, 1950).

30. This by no means has to entail an ethical concern for the betterment of human life in society – as for example, the so-called

Arthashastras (treatises on the management of social affairs, written primarily for the use of princes) eloquently testify.

31. J. Bernhart (ed.), *Theologia germanica* (New York, Pantheon, 1949), p. 159; (London, Victor Gollancz, 1950).

32. cf. Eric Voegelin, *Israel and Revelation* (Baton Rouge, Louisiana State University Press, 1956).

33. cf. R. de Vaux, *Les institutions de l'Ancien Testament* (Paris, Editions du Cerf, 1961), Vol. I, pp. 141ff.; *Ancient Israel: Its Life and Institutions*, trans. John McHugh (London, Danton Longmans & Todd, 1961).

34. I have tried to make this point in my *The Precarious Vision* (Garden City, N.Y., Doubleday, 1961), pp. 219ff.

35. 'Dans son ensemble la perspective biblique n'est pas dirigée vers la conservation du monde, mais vers sa transformation.' Edmond Jacob, *Théologie de l'Ancien Testament* (Neuchâtel, Delachaux & Niestlé, 1955), p. 184.

36. I am indebted to Anton Zijderveld for this very suggestive term. *Vide* Appendix II for a further discussion of this.

Chapter 5

1. cf. Hermann Luebbe, *Saekularisierung—Geschichte eines ideen-politischen Begriffs* (Freiburg, Alber, 1965).

2. cf. ibid., *passim*.

3. cf. for instance, Olof Klohr (ed.), *Religion und Atheismus heute* (Berlin, Deutscher Verlag der Wissenschaften, 1966), with Sabino Acquaviva, *L'eclissi del sacro nella civiltà industriale* (Milan, Edizioni Communità, 1961).

4. cf. E. Bethge (ed.), *Die muendige Welt*, Vols. 1–2 (Munich, Kaiser, 1955–6). For a recent statement of a similar viewpoint, though expressed in a more Barthian context, cf. Arnold Loen, *Saekularisation* (Munich, Kaiser, 1965). The positive Christian evaluation of 'secularity' has recently been popularized in America by Harvey Cox, *The Secular City* (New York, Macmillan, and London, S.C.M. Press, 1965). For a more sociologically oriented statement of this Christian position, cf. Dietrich von Oppen, *Das personale Zeitalter* (Stuttgart, Kreuz, 1960).

5. cf. Joachim Matthes, *Die Emigration der Kirche aus der Gesellschaft* (Hamburg, Furche, 1964); also, cf. the contributions by Trutz Rendtorff and David Martin in the *International Yearbook for the Sociology of Religion*, 2 (1966).

6. This point gains poignancy if one reflects on the prominence of Weber's work in this discussion. Anyone who cites Weber in this context should certainly recall his understanding of the ironic relationship between human intentions and their historical consequences!

7. Probably the largest amount of data on the social differentiation of religious identification has been collected by Gabriel LeBras and those (mainly Catholic sociologists) who have followed his methods. cf. his *Etudes de sociologie religieuse* (Paris, Presses Universitaires de France, 1955). Also, cf. Emile Pin, *Pratique religieuse et classes sociales* (Paris, Spes, 1956), and F. A. Isambert, *Christianisme et classe ouvrière* (Tournai, Casterman, 1961). The works of Joseph Fichter, beginning with *Southern Parish* (Chicago, Chicago University Press, 1951), reflect a very similar orientation in American Catholic sociology. The classical work dealing with this general problematic in the sociology of religion in America is Richard Niebuhr, *The Social Sources of Denominationalism* (New York, Holt, 1929), which has stimulated a number of empirical case studies. For a recent example, cf. N. J. Demerath, *Social Class in American Protestantism* (Chicago, Rand McNally, 1965). The most thorough study of its kind in America is probably Gerhard Lenski, *The Religious Factor* (Garden City, N.Y., Doubleday, 1961).

8. This has been succinctly summarized by Thomas Luckmann: 'Dagegen ist aus den Forschungsergebnissen zu entnehmen, dass Kirchlichkeit zu einem Randphaenomen in der modernen Gesellschaft geworden ist. In Europa charakterisiert Kirchlichkeit nur einen geringen Bruchteil der Bevoelkerung, und zwar bezeichnenderweise jenen Teil, der selbst sozusagen am Rand der modernen Gesellschaftsentwicklung steht, so vor allem die Bauern, das Kleinbuergertum, die Ueberbleibsel "staendischer" Herkunft innerhalb der Mittelschicht, die noch nicht in den Arbeitsprozess Eingeschalteten oder die aus dem Arbeitsprozess schon Ausgeschalteten' (*Das Problem der Religion in der modernen Gesellschaft* [Freiburg, Rombach, 1963], p. 29). Also cf. Reinhard Koester, *Die Kirchentreuen* (Stuttgart, Enke, 1959).

9. This point has also been stated very well by Luckmann, op. cit. For secularization *within* institutional religion in America, cf. Will Herberg, *Protestant − Catholic − Jew* (Garden City, N.Y., Doubleday, 1955), and my *The Noise of Solemn Assemblies* (Garden City, N.Y., Doubleday, 1961).

10. cf. Daniel Lerner, *The Passing of Traditional Society* (Glencoe, Ill., Free Press, 1958; London, Collier-Macmillan, 1964); Robert Bellah (ed.), *Religion and Progress in Modern Asia* (New York, Free Press 1965); Donald Smith (ed.), *South Asian Politics and Religion* (Princeton, Princeton University Press, 1966).

11. While the material accumulated by Catholic sociologists mainly concerns the institutional aspects of secularization (particularly as expressed in the externals of religious practice), a good many data on the subjective correlates of this may also be found here. cf. Acquaviva, op. cit., for a summary, as well as Hervé Carrier, *Psychosociologie de l'appartenance religieuse* (Rome, Presses de l'Université Grégorienne, 1960). Also cf. Gordon Allport, *The Individual and His Religion* (New York, Macmillan, 1950; London, Constable, 1951); Hans-Otto Woelber, *Religion ohne Entscheidung* (Goettingen, Vandenhoeck & Ruprecht, 1959); Rose Goldsen *et al.*, *What College Students Think* (Princeton, Van Nostrand, 1960).

12. On the latter possibility, cf. Eberhard Stammler, *Protestanten ohne Kirche* (Stuttgart, Kreuz, 1960).

13. The term 'carrier' (*Traeger*) is used here in a Weberian sense.

14. cf. Klohr, op. cit. For a nice comparison with recent data from an emphatically non-socialist context, cf. Ramón Bayés, *Los ingenieros, la sociedad y la religión* (Barcelona, Fontanella, 1965). The comparison would have entertained Veblen!

15. Both these points, of course, are crucial to an understanding of Weber's work in this area and in the sociology of religion generally.

16. The following summation closely follows Weber, particularly his *The Protestant Ethic and the Spirit of Capitalism*, trans. Talcott Parsons (London, Allen & Unwin, 1930). Also, cf. Ernst Troeltsch, *Die Bedeutung des Protestantismus fuer die Entstehung der modernen Welt* (1911); Karl Holl, 'Die Kulturbedeutung der Reformation', in his *Gesammelte Aufsaetze zur Kirchengeschichte*, Vol. 1 (1932); *The Cultural Significance of the Reformation* (New York, Meridian Books, 1959). For a linkage of this with the problematic of secularization, cf. Howard Becker, 'Saekularisationsprozesse', *Koelner Vierteljahreshefte fuer Soziologie* (1932), 283ff. and 450ff.

17. Weber – 'Entzauberung der Welt'.

18. This point is made, quite explicitly, in Weber's *Ancient Judaism*, although the term 'secularized' occurs only once (albeit in an interesting place, where Weber discusses the effect of the cen-

tralization of the cult in Jerusalem on the religious significance of the clan). But Weber's main interest in the Old Testament was in a related but different question – namely, that of the development of the Jewish economic ethic and its relationship (minimal, he thought) with the origins of modern capitalism. All the same, Weber's work on the Old Testament is of great importance for our present question as well. Biblical scholars have repeatedly pointed out the 'desacralizing' and 'demythologizing' tendencies of the Old Testament, at least since Wellhausen (who spoke of 'denaturalization' in comparing Israel with the surrounding Near Eastern religions). For a very clear statement of this view (though geared to a theological rather than historical purpose), cf. Friedrich Gogarten, *Verhaengnis und Hoffnung der Neuzeit* (1953).

19. cf. Henri Frankfort, *et al.*, *The Intellectual Adventure of Ancient Man* (Chicago, University of Chicago Press, 1964), and *Kingship and the Gods* (Chicago, University of Chicago Press, 1948); Eric Voegelin, *Israel and Revelation* (Baton Rouge, Louisiana State University Press, 1956).

20. This term is taken from Voegelin.

21. cf. Mircea Eliade, *Cosmos and History* (New York, Harper, 1959); *Myth and Reality* (London, Allen & Unwin, 1964).

22. The term 'cosmization' is taken from Eliade.

23. James Pritchard (ed.), *Ancient Near Eastern Texts* (Princeton, Princeton University Press, 1955), p. 5. For a commentary of this fascinating text, cf. John Wilson, *The Burden of Egypt* (Chicago, University of Chicago Press, 1951).

24. The last of these three terms is taken from Weber. The terms 'rationalization' and 'rationality' are understood in a Weberian sense throughout. For our general view of Israelite religion, cf. Edmond Jacob, *Théologie de l'Ancien Testament* (Neuchâtel, Delachaux & Niestlé, 1955); Voegelin, op. cit., Gerhard von Rad, *Theologie des alten Testaments*, Vols. 1–2 (Munich, Kaiser, 1957 and 1960).

25. Most of these points were explicitly made by Weber. Indeed, amazingly little has to be added to Weber's picture of the Israelite conception of God, despite the much wider knowledge of the general Near Eastern context since then. For more recent discussions of the early history of Yahwism, cf. Albrecht Alt, *Der Gott der Vaeter* (1929), and Samuel Nyström, *Beduinentum und Jahwismus* (1946).

26. cf. Hermann Gunkel, *Genesis* (1917), and Gerhard von Rad, *Das erste Buch Mose* (1950). The text of the Enuma Elish may be found in Pritchard, op. cit. Also, cf. Anne-Marie Esnoul; *et al., La naissaice du monde* (Paris, Editions du Seuil, 1959).

27. cf. Artur Weiser, *Glaube und Geschichte im alten Testament* (1931); Edmond Jacob, *La tradition historique en Israël* (1946); C. R. North, *The Old Testament Interpretation of History* (London, Epworth Press, 1946). The same understanding of the historicity of the entire Old Testament is elaborated in great detail in the already cited work of von Rad's, *Theologie des alten Testaments*, particularly in Vol 1. Also, cf. Oscar Cullmann, *Christ et le temps* (Neuchâtel, Delachaux & Niestlé, 1947); *Christ and Time*, trans. Floyd V. Filson (London, S.C.M. Press, 1951).

28. The following account is closely dependent on Weber. On the relationship of Israelite ethics and Israelite history, cf. Adolphe Lods, *Les prophètes d'Israël et les débuts du judaïsme* (1935); *The Prophets and the Rise of Judaism*, trans. S. H. Hooke (London, Kegan Paul, 1937); and Adolphe Causse, *Du groupe ethnique à la communauté religieuse* (1937).

29. In our view of the historical role of Christianity we are, again, heavily dependent on Weber. Our understanding of the relationship of Christianity to the mythological cosmos on the one hand and to Judaism on the other has been strongly influenced by Rudolf Bultmann. cf. not only his writings on 'demythologization', but also his *Theology of the New Testament* (London, S.C.M. Press, 1952), as well as his *Das Urchristentum* Zurich, Artemis, 1949). Also, cf. Gogarten, op. cit.

30. Again, our dependence on Weber is obvious here. Also, cf. Ernst Troeltsch, *Die Soziallehren der christlichen Kirchen* (1911); *The Social Teaching of the Christian Churches*, trans. Olive Wyon (London, Allen & Unwin, 1931).

31. This point has been excellently stated by Luckmann, op. cit.

32. cf. Troeltsch, *Die Soziallehren*, as well as the discussion of Lutheranism in Weber's *The Protestant Ethic and the Spirit of Capitalism*.

33. cf. Montgomery Watt, *Islam and the Integration of Society* (Evanston, Northwestern University Press, 1961), and Reuben Levy, *The Social Structure of Islam* (Cambridge, Cambridge University Press, 1957). The highly intriguing question of the general relationship of Islam to secularization cannot, of course, be pursued here.

Chapter 6

1. The main points in this chapter were made before in Peter Berger and Thomas Luckmann, 'Secularization and Pluralism', *International Yearbook for the Sociology of Religion* (1966), 73ff. On the narrower question of pluralism and ecumenicity, cf. my 'A Market Model for the Analysis of Ecumenicity', *Social Research* (Spring 1963), 77ff. My view of the social psychology of contemporary religion is heavily indebted to Thomas Luckmann. cf. his *Das Problem der Religion in der modernen Gesellschaft* (Freiburg, Rombach, 1963 – English version, *The Invisible Religion* [New York, Macmillan, 1971]).

2. It is in this way that the Marxian and Weberian conceptions of religion can be integrated theoretically, at least on the level of general theory (that is, bracketing specific contradictions of historical interpretation) and provided one differentiates between Marx and doctrinaire Marxism.

3. Weber's theory of charisma and the routinization of charisma provides a model for this kind of differentiated analysis. cf. my 'The Sociological Study of Sectarianism', *Social Research* (Winter 1954), 467ff.

4. For a discussion of this in the sociologically peculiar case of American Protestantism, cf. my *The Noise of Solemn Assemblies* (Garden City, N.Y., Doubleday, 1961).

5. The category of rationalization is, again, applied here in a Weberian sense.

6. On this, cf. Dennison Nash and Peter Berger, 'The Child, the Family and the Religious Revival in Suburbia', *Journal for the Scientific Study of Religion* (Fall 1962), 85ff.

7. On the general phenomenon of public and private spheres in modern society, cf. Arnold Gehlen, *Die Seele im technischen Zeitalter* (Hamburg, Rowohlt, 1957); Luckmann, op. cit.; Juergen Habermas, *Strukturwandel der Oeffentlichkeit* (Neuwied/Rhein, Luchterhand, 1962).

8. This definition of the denomination was first made by H. Richard Niebuhr in his *The Social Sources of Denominationalism* (1929).

9. cf. H. Godin and Y. Daniel, *France, pays de mission?* (Paris, Cerf, 1943); *France, a Missionary Land*, trans. M. Ward (London, Sheed & Ward, 1949). Also, cf. Adrien Dansette, *Destin du catholicisme français* (Paris, Flammarion, 1957).

10. In view of the pervasiveness of bureaucracy on the contemporary religious scene and the general acknowledgement of this by those involved in it, it is remarkable how little attention has been given to it by sociology-of-religion research as compared, for instance, with the attention lavished on the local parish. One plausible explanation of this is the fact that so much of this research has been sponsored by the religious bureaucracies themselves, whose pragmatic interest was precisely in the achievement of their goals 'on the outside', *not* in reflection about their *own* functionality. For one of the very few studies of religious bureaucracy, cf. Paul Harrison, *Authority and Power in the Free Church Tradition* (Princeton, Princeton University Press, 1959). For a discussion of some economic aspects of this, cf. F. Ernest Johnson and J. Emory Ackerman, *The Church as Employer, Money Raiser and Investor* (New York, Harper, 1959).

11. cf. Hans Gerth and C. Wright Mills, *Character and Social Structure* (New York, Harcourt, Brace, 1953), especially pp. 165ff.; (London, Routledge & Kegan Paul, 1954).

12. cf. my 'Religious Establishment and Theological Education', *Theology Today* (July 1962), 178ff.

13. cf. Robert Lee, *The Social Sources of Church Unity* (New York, Abingdon, 1960). Lee describes these developments very well, but with little awareness of their underlying socio-economic forces.

14. cf. Yves Congar, *Jalons pour une théologie du laïcat* (Paris, Cerf, 1953), which marks a decisive change in Catholic thinking on this matter.

15. cf. Lee, op. cit., pp. 188ff.

16. The following discussion is based on Gehlen's general theory of modern 'subjectivization', developed particularly in his previously cited *Die Seele im technischen Zeitalter*. For the application of this approach to the sociology of contemporary religion, cf. Helmut Schelsky, 'Ist die Dauerreflektion institutionalisierbar?' *Zeitschrift fuer evangelische Ethik*, 1957: 4, and Luckman, op. cit. For an empirical study of 'opinion religion', cf. Hans-Otto Woelber, *Religion ohne Entscheidung* (Goettingen, Vandenhoeck & Ruprecht, 1959).

17. cf. my 'Towards a Sociological Understanding of Psycho-analysis', *Social Research* (Spring 1965), 26ff.

Chapter 7

1. On the general development of Protestant theology, the classical works on the history of dogma of Albrecht Ritschl and Adolf von Harnack continue to be essential. On the development since Schleiermacher, cf. H. R. Mackintosh, *Types of Modern Theology* (London, Nisbet, 1937); Karl Barth, *Die protestantische Theologie im 19 Jahrhundert* (1947); Horst Stephan and Martin Schmidt, *Geschichte der deutschen evangelischen Theologie* (1960).
2. cf. Stephen and Schmidt, op. cit., pp. 92ff.
3. cf. ibid., pp. 316ff.
4. cf. Heinrich Hermelink (ed.), *Kirche im Kampf* (Tuebingen, Wunderlich, 1950). For a sociological discussion of the relationship of various factions of German Protestantism in this struggle, cf. my 'Religious Liberalism and the Totalitarian Situation', *Hartford Seminary Foundation Bulletin* (March 1960), 3ff.
5. This point has been made by Jermann Luebbe, *Saekularisierung* (Freiburg, Alber, 1965), pp. 117ff.
6. For a compendium of this debate over a period of years, cf. Hans Bartsch (ed.), *Kerygma und Mythos*, Vols. 1–4 (Hamburg, Reich, 1948–55).
7. Paul Tillich, *Systematic Theology*, Vols. 1–3 (Chicago, University of Chicago Press, 1951–63; London, Nisbet, 1953).
8. Friedrich Gogarten, *Verhaengnis und Hoffnung der Neuzeit* (Stuttgart, Vorwerk, 1953). For a useful introduction to Gogarten's work, cf. Larry Shiner, *The Secularization of History* (Nashville, Abingdon, 1966).
9. cf. Eberhard Bethge (ed.), *Die muendige Welt*, Vols. 1–2 (Munich, Kaiser, 1955–6); Martin Marty (ed.), *The Place of Bonhoeffer* (New York, Association Press, 1962; London, S.C.M. Press, 1963).
10. Wolfhart Pannenberg (ed.), *Offenbarung als Geschichte* (Goettingen, Vandenhoeck & Ruprecht, 1963).
11. John Robinson, *Honest to God* (London, S.C.M. Press, 1963).
12. For a useful compendium of the latter, cf. Thomas Altizer and William Hamilton, *Radical Theology and the Death of God* (Indianapolis, Bobbs-Merrill, 1966).
13. Harvey Cox, *The Secular City* (New York, Macmillan, and London, S.C.M. Press, 1965).
14. cf. Louis Schneider and Sanford Dornbusch, *Popular Religion*

(Chicago, University of Chicago Press, 1958); Samuel Klausner, *Psychiatry and Religion* (New York, Free Press, and London, Collier-Macmillan, 1964).

Subject Index

Index of Names

Penguinews and Penguins in Print

Every month we issue an illustrated magazine, *Penguinews*. It's a lively guide to all the latest Penguins, Pelicans and Puffins, and always contains an article on a major Penguin author, plus other features of contemporary interest.

Penguinews is supplemented by *Penguins in Print*, a complete list of all the available Penguin titles – there are now over four thousand!

The cost is no more than the postage; so why not write for a free copy of this month's *Penguinews*? And if you'd like both publications sent for a year, just send us a cheque or a postal order for 30p (if you live in the United Kingdom) or 60p (if you live elsewhere), and we'll put you on our mailing list.

Dept EP, Penguin Books Ltd,
Harmondsworth, Middlesex

Note: *Penguinews* and *Penguins in Print* are not available in the U.S.A. or Canada.

Invitation to Sociology

A Humanistic Perspective

'Unlike puppets,' writes Professor Berger, 'we have the possibility of stopping in our movements, looking up and perceiving the machinery by which we have been moved. In this act lies the first step towards freedom.'

Sociology is defined as 'the science of the development and nature and laws of human society': but what is its purpose? Without belittling its scientific procedures, Professor Berger stresses the humanistic affinity of sociology with history and philosophy. It is a discipline which encourages a fuller awareness of the human world . . . to the purpose of bettering it.

The author's comments on the social institutions which men have shaped and on the men whom these institutions, in their turn, have moulded (together with his outline of the contributions of such major sociologists as Weber, Durkheim, Veblen and Mead, among others) clearly and often wittily tell the reader just what sociology is, and define the larger purpose of this social self-consciousness.

Not for sale in the U.S.A. or Canada

The Social Construction of Reality

Peter L. Berger and Thomas Luckmann

This book is concerned with the sociology of 'everything that passes for knowledge in society', and particularly with that 'common-sense knowledge' that constitutes the reality of everyday life for the ordinary member of society. The authors are concerned to present an analysis of knowledge in everyday life in the context of a theory of society as a dialectical process between objective and subjective reality. Their development of a theory of institutions, legitimation and socialization has implications beyond the discipline of sociology, and their 'humanistic' approach has considerable relevance for other social scientists, historians, philosophers and anthropologists.

'. . . a serious, open-minded book upon a serious subject.'
Julius Gould, *The Listener*.

Thomas Luckmann is Professor of Sociology at the University of Frankfurt

Not for sale in the U.S.A.